GOOD HOUSEKEEPING

K·N·I·T·T·I·N·G
I·N S·T·Y·L·E

GOOD HOUSEKEEPING

GOOD HOUSEKEEPING

K·N·I·T·T·I·N·G

I·N S·T·Y·L·E

CONSULTANT EDITOR Angela Kennedy

PHOTOGRAPHER Nick Briggs

 Pan Books

Published by

The National Magazine Company Limited   and   Pan Books Limited
National Magazine House   18/21 Cavaye Place
72 Broadwick Street   London SW10 9PG
London W1V 2BP

First impression 1985

Copyright © 1985 by The National Magazine Company Limited

ISBN 0 330 28939 X (paperback)
ISBN 0 330 29192 0 (hardback)

Edited by: Laurine Croasdale
Design Consultant: Debbie Bliss
Illustrations by: Tina Clark
Designed by: Harry Green

Assistant stylist: Sharon Ashworth
Hair: Joel O'Sullivan for Schumi
Make up: Helen Jeffers

Location: The Dingle Peninsula, County Kerry, Ireland
Flights arranged through Aer Lingus ♣, internal
transport with Dan Dooley's car hire, Shannon Airport

Filmset by Advanced Filmsetters (Glasgow) Ltd
Printed in Spain by Printer IGSA   Barcelona   D.L.B. 21216-1985

CONTENTS

INTRODUCTION

Most books on handknitting cover the craft, the skills and traditions but of the dozens that get published each year, there has never been one that has interested me enough to knit more than just *one* of the designs featured.

This is to be the exception. Here are thirty designs you'll just long to knit. *Good Housekeeping Knitting in Style* is the ultimate book of patterns to appeal to the traditionalist who likes handknits with a timeless quality. There are no jazzy 'fun' picture knits, no frivolous throw-away gimmicks, just wonderful modern classics with a long lasting lifespan that sets them apart from fast changing fashion fads. *Knitting in Style* amply illustrated, creams the classics and spans the generations.

We don't intend to baffle you with science and the history of knitting, but to present to you our own personal choice of thirty fabulous designs skilfully originated by Debbie Bliss, Louise Parsons, Tina Clark and Mary Norden, whose work often appears in the pages of Good Housekeeping's own popular handknit features. This is an extension of these fashion pages. Stylish handknits that need very little extra help from accessories to make them work in the world of fashion. For first time knitters there are some easy quick-to-knit styles and for dab hands there are the intricacies of exciting fancy Fair Isles.

Knitting in Style is the best of traditional patterns for fashion purists. It's for people who enjoy knitting to create something individual and not particularly because knitting can make it cheaper. We've combed the spinners for the loveliest of natural yarns wherever possible using pure wool, cotton, mohair and silk. For why go to all that time and trouble to create something that will not stand the test of time? These designs, these yarns and this book does just that. Happy Knitting in Style.

Angela Kennedy

BASIC INFORMATION

The flow of yarn which is controlled by the knitter is known as tension, and is as personal as handwriting. Some knitters put more stress on the yarn, making a smaller stitch and tighter knitted fabric; others put less stress on the yarn and make a looser fabric. For this reason a tension sample is essential for the success of your finished garment.

Why stitch gauge is important
You must always measure stitch gauge before you start to make anything. This is necessary for two reasons: to check your tension against stitch gauge given in a pattern, and to calculate the number of stitches to cast on and rows to work when you are planning a design of your own. The stitch gauge or tension is always given at the beginning of a pattern and states the number of stitches and rows to the centimetre or inch using the yarn, needles and stitch pattern for a given design.

Calculating the number of stitches and rows is known as stitch gauging. Three factors influence stitch gauge:
1 The size of needles and type of yarn.
2 The type of stitch pattern.
3 The knitter.

Making a stitch gauge sample
Use the same yarn, needles and stitch pattern as those to be used for the main work. Knit a sample at least 12.5 × 12.5 cm/5 × 5 ins square. Smooth out the finished sample on a flat surface but do not stretch it.

Measuring the number of stitches
This determines the width of the knitting. Place a steel ruler or tape measure across the sample and mark 10 cm/4 ins across with pins. Count the number of stitches between the pins. For complete accuracy, pin out the sample several times. An extra half stitch will prove to be vital when you are working from a knitting pattern or when you are gauging the number of stitches to cast on for your own design.

Adjusting stitch gauge
The stitch gauge can be adjusted by changing the size of needles and working another sample. If there are too many stitches to the centimetre or to the inch, your tension is too tight and you should change to needles a size larger. If there are too few stitches, your tension is too loose and you should change to needles a size smaller. If the number of stitches is correct but the number of rows incorrect, check the length as you proceed with the pattern.

Measuring the number of rows
This determines the depth of the knitting. The stitch gauge also determines the number of rows to the centimetre or to the inch. Place a ruler vertically along the fabric and mark out 10 cm/4 ins with pins. Count the number of rows between the pins. From this count you can gauge the number of rows needed to reach the planned length of a design. You can also calculate where shaping is required and the position of increases and decreases.

Altering a pattern
Always make a stitch gauge sample if you intend to alter a pattern for example, changing from stocking stitch to a lace stitch, or adding a cable panel. Also check the stitch gauge when changing from a single colour to a multicolour pattern.

Garment care
A knitted garment will have a much longer life and better appearance if it is properly cared for. Always look on the ball band and check instructions for cleaning and pressing. Where the garment should be handwashed, wash in lukewarm water using a soap especially designed for knitwear. Do not leave to soak. Immerse garment and squeeze it gently, avoiding wringing or rubbing. Rinse thoroughly in tepid water, then gently squeeze to remove all excess water. Hold the garment at all times otherwise the weight will pull it out of shape. Place a towel on a table and dry the garment flat, patting it into shape. Dry away from direct heat.

NOT QUITE CRICKET

Deep V-necked
sweater with
cables and colour
(see page 44)

COUNTRY
TWEED

Cable detailed
sweater in a soft
tweedy yarn
(see page 45)

RED
SUMMER
SIZZLER

A bright cotton
knit in a shell stitch
pattern
(see page 46)

FAIR ISLE GOES FLUFFY

A boxy cardigan in
a Fair Isle mixture
of pastels and
brights
(see page 47)

STORMY SWEATER

Monochromatic his/hers with classic cross-over collar (see page 49)

A WISP
OF WHITE

Luxurious angora
sweater with lace
diamonds,
bobbles and
cables
(see page 50)

BUTTONS AND BOWS

A collared,
jacquard jacket
with rows of bows
(see page 51)

NEATLY
NAVY

A smart textured
slipover with a
dash of Fair Isle
(see page 53)

STEPPING SIDEWAYS

Take knits in a new
direction by
cabling sideways
from a central
panel
(see page 54)

BEATING
THE BLUES

Lagoon blue
cotton knit with a
centre cable
(see page 55)

STYLISH AND SPORTY

A winter warmer
in a bright Aran
yarn
(see page 56)

RIBBON
SINGLET

A quick, easy knit
in a mesh-style
stitch
(see page 57)

SOFT IMPRESSIONS

A cool summer
cardi in honey-
coloured mohair
(see page 58)

COOL
COTTON

A textured tunic
top with a slit neck
(see page 59)

FAIR ISLE
WITH FLAIR

A pencil-slim Fair
Isle with a feel for
the 30's
(see page 60)

A CLASSIC IN CREAM

A sleeveless top in
an Aran blend of
bobbles and moss
stitch
(see page 62)

TASTEFULLY
TEXTURED

A chunky winter
top with a
travelling cable
stitch
(see page 63)

DIVERTING DIAGONALS

A two-tone crew
neck sweater
worked in moss
stitch
(see page 64)

A SAMPLER
FOR SPRING

A subtle
patchwork of knit
and purl stitches
(see page 65)

LONG AND LANGUOROUS

A Fred Perry shirt-style sweater with a hint of a tint on collar and cuffs (see page 66)

NEW-WAVE NORWEGIAN

A striking ski-
sweater in black
and cream
(see page 67)

SIMPLY
SUMMER

A summer top in
lacy cables
(see page 68)

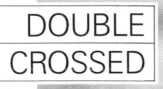

DOUBLE
CROSSED

A low double-
breasted jacket
with deep welts
(see page 69)

MOHAIR
MAGIC

Stunning simple
mohair cowl
(see page 71)

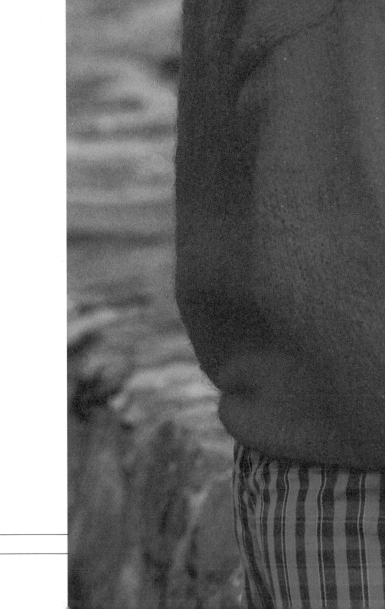

SKINNY RIB

Figure hugging
60's style top
(see page 72)

ZANY ZIG ZAGS

Longline jacket in jacquard zig zags
(see page 73)

SOFTLY CABLED

Generous cabled
slipover in a
mohair mix
(see page 74)

FINELY FEMININE

A 40's style in fine-
knit 4-ply
(see page 75)

LEAN AND LINEN LOOK

Simple sleeveless
top with 3-button
front tab
(see page 77)

SITTING
PRETTY

Delicate diamonds
in a punchy pink
(see page 78)

NOT QUITE CRICKET

Materials

16(17:18) 50 g balls of *Sunbeam Pure New Wool DK* in main colour M.
1(2:2) balls in 1st contrast colour B.
1(1:1) ball in each of 3 contrast colours A, C, D.
1 pair each of 3¼ mm (No. 10) and 4 mm (No. 8) knitting needles.
1 cable needle.

Measurements

Bust	86(91:97) cm	34(36:38) ins
Length	73 cm	28¾ ins
Sleeve Seam	45 cm	17¾ ins

Tension 28 sts and 30 rows to 10 cm over cable patt on 4 mm needles.

Abbreviations Alt-alternate; beg-beginning; cm-centimetres; cont-continue; dec-decrease; foll-following; ins-inches; inc-increase; K-knit; m 1-pick up loop lying between sts and work into the back of it; patt-pattern; P-purl; rem-remain; rep-repeat; sl-slip; st(s)-stitch(es); st st-stocking stitch; tbl-through the back of the loops; tog-together.
T3L-sl next st to cable needle to front of work, K2, then K1 from cable needle.
T3R-sl next 2 sts to cable needle to back of work, K1, then K2 from cable needle.

Note When working in Fair Isle' patt, strand yarn not in use loosely across wrong side of work.

BACK

With 3¼ mm needles and M, cast on 127(133:139) sts.
1st row (right side) K1, [P1, K1] to end.
2nd row P1, [K1, P1] to end.
Rep the last 2 rows until work measures 8 cm/3¼ ins from beg, ending with a 1st row.
Next row Rib 5(6:2), inc in next st, [rib 8(7:8), inc in next st] 13(15:15) times, rib to end. 141(149:155) sts.
Change to 4 mm needles and beg with a K row, work 2 rows in st st.
Cont in patt as folls:
1st row K1(2:2) M, [1A, 2M] to last 2(0:0) sts, 1(0:0) A, 1(0:0) M.
2nd row P0(0:1) B, 2(0:2) M, [1M, 3B, 2M] to last 1(5:2) sts, 1M, 0(3:1) B, 0(1:0) M.
3rd row K1(2:2) B, [1M, 2B] to last 2(0:0) sts, 1(0:0) M, 1(0:0) B.
4th row P1(0:0) C, 1(0:0) D, [2C, 1D] to last 1(2:2) sts, 1(2:2) C.
5th row As 3rd row.
6th row As 2nd row.
7th row As 1st row.
Beg with a P row, work 3 rows in st st, using M only.
11th row P1(5:8), [T3R, P1, T3L, P5] to last 8(12:15) sts, T3R, P1, T3L, P to end.
12th row K1(5:8), [P3, K1, P3, K5] to last 8(12:15) sts, P3, K1, P3, K to end.
Rep the last 2 rows twice more, then the 11th row again.
18th row K1(5:8), [P7, K5] to last 8(12:15) sts, P7, K to end.
19th row P1(5:8), [K7, P5] to last 8(12:15) sts, K7, P to end.
Rep the last 2 rows twice more.
24th row As 18th row.
Rep 11th–24th rows once more, **but** reading T3L instead of T3R and T3R instead of T3L.
Rep 11th–24th rows once more.
Rep 11th–17th rows once more, **but** reading T3L instead of T3R and T3R instead of T3L.
60th row With M, P to end.
These 60 rows form the patt and are rep throughout. Cont in patt until 118 rows have been worked in patt, thus ending with a wrong-side row.

Shape Armholes

Keeping patt correct, cast off 19(21:22) sts at beg of next 2 rows. 103(107:111) sts.
Cont without shaping until armholes measure 25 cm/9¾ ins, ending with a wrong-side row.

Shape Shoulders

Cast off 28(30:32) sts at beg of next 2 rows.
Leave rem 47 sts on a holder.

FRONT

Work as given for Back until work measures 39 cm/15¼ ins from beg, ending with a wrong-side row.

Divide for Neck

Keeping patt correct;
Next row Patt 70(74:77), turn and leave rem sts on a spare needle.
Next row Patt to end.
Dec one st at end of next and every foll 4th row until work measures the same as Back to Armholes, ending with a wrong-side row.

Shape Armhole

Cont to dec at neck edge on every 4th row as set, **at the same time**, cast off 19(21:22) sts at beg of next row.
Keeping armhole edge straight, cont to dec at neck edge only until 28(30:32) sts rem.
Cont without shaping until armhole measures the same as on Back, ending with a wrong-side row.
Cast off.
Return to the sts on spare needle; with right side facing, sl first st on to a safety pin, rejoin yarn and patt to end.
Cont to match first side reversing shaping.

SLEEVES

With 3¼ mm needles and M, cast on 55(57:59) sts and work in rib as on Back for 8 cm/3¼ ins, ending with a 1st row.
Next row Rib 9(11:13), m 1, [rib 1, m 1] 37(35:33) times, rib to end. 93 sts.
Change to 4 mm needles and beg with a K row, work 2 rows in st st.
Cont in patt as folls:
1st row K 1M, [1A, 2M] to last 2 sts, 1A, 1M.
2nd row P [3M, 3B] to last 3 sts, 3M.
Cont in patt as set, to match Back, inc one st at each end of the next and every foll 6th row, working the inc sts into reverse st st on cable patt and colours on Fair Isle patt, until there are 107 sts, then on every foll 4th row until there are 141 sts.
Work 1 row placing a marker at each end of row.
Work 20(22:24) rows, then cast off **loosely**.

NECKBAND

Join right shoulder seam.
With 3¼ mm needles, M and right side facing, pick up and K 111 sts evenly down left front neck, K front neck st from safety pin, pick up and K 110 sts evenly up right front neck, then K back neck sts. 269 sts.
1st row Work in K1, P1 rib to 2 sts before centre front st, K2 tog, P1, K2 tog tbl rib to end.
2nd row Rib to 2 sts before centre front st, P2 tog tbl, K1, P2 tog, rib to end.
Rep the last 2 rows twice more, then the 1st row again.
Cast off in rib, still dec at centre front.

TO MAKE UP

Press work according to instructions on ball band.
Join left shoulder and neckband seam. Sew in sleeves, sewing the rows above markers to the cast off sts at underarms. Join side and sleeve seams.
Press seams.

COUNTRY TWEED

Materials
19(20:21) 50 g balls of *Sirdar Nomad*.
1 pair each of 5 mm (No. 6) and 6½ mm (No. 3) knitting needles.
Set of four 5 mm and 6½ mm double pointed needles.
1 cable needle.

Measurements
Bust	86(91:97) cm	34(36:38) ins
Length	62(64:66) cm	24½(25¼:26) ins
Sleeve Seam	43 cm	17 ins

Tension 14 sts and 19 rows to 10 cm over st st on 6½ mm needles.

Abbreviations Alt-alternate; beg-beginning; cm-centimetres; cont-continue; dec-decrease; foll-following; ins-inches; inc-increase; K-knit; patt-pattern; P-purl; rem-remain; rep-repeat; sl-slip; st(s)-stitch(es); st st-stocking stitch.
C4-sl next 2 sts to cable needle to back of work, K2, then K2 from cable needle.
C8-sl next 4 sts to cable needle to back of work, K4, then K4 from cable needle.

BACK
With 5 mm needles cast on 73(77:81) sts.
1st row (right side) K1, [P1, K1] to end.
2nd row P1, [K1, P1] to end.
Rep the last 2 rows until work measures 8 cm/3¼ ins from beg, ending with a 1st row.
Next row Rib 4(6:8), inc in next st, [rib 1, inc in next st] 32 times, rib to end. 106(110:114) sts.
Change to 6½ mm needles and cont in patt as folls:
1st row P10(11:12), [K4, P3, K8, P3, K4, P10(11:12)] 3 times.
2nd and every foll alt row K10(11:12), [P4, K3, P8, K3, P4, K10(11:12)] 3 times.
3rd row P10(11:12), [C4, P3, K8, P3, C4, P10(11:12)] 3 times.

5th row As 1st row.
7th row P10(11:12), [C4, P3, C8, P3, C4, P10(11:12)] 3 times.
8th row As 2nd row.
These 8 rows form the patt and are rep throughout. Cont in patt until work measures 40(41:42) cm/15¾(16¼:16½) ins from beg, ending with a wrong-side row.
Shape Armholes
Keeping patt correct, cast off 14(15:16) sts at beg of next 2 rows. 78(80:82) sts.
Cont without shaping until armholes measure 22(23:24) cm/8¾(9:9½) ins, ending with a wrong-side row.
Shape Shoulders
Cast off 7(7:8) sts at beg of next 4 rows, then 8(9:8) sts at beg of next 2 rows.
Leave rem 34 sts on a holder.

FRONT
Work as given for Back until armholes measure 13(14:15) cm/5(5½:6) ins, ending with a wrong-side row.
Shape Neck
Keeping patt correct;
Next row Patt 27(28:29), turn and leave rem sts on a spare needle.
Dec one st at beg of next and foll 4 alt rows. 22(23:24) sts.
Cont without shaping until armhole measures the same as on Back, ending with a wrong-side row.
Shape Shoulder
Cast off 7(7:8) sts at beg of next and foll alt row. Work one row, then cast off rem 8(9:8) sts.
Return to the sts on spare needle; with right side facing, sl first 24 sts on to a holder, rejoin yarn and patt to end.
Cont to match first side, reversing shaping.

SLEEVES
With 5 mm needles cast on 41(43:45) sts and work in rib as on Back for 10 cm/4 ins, ending with a 1st row.
Next row Rib 4, inc in next st, [rib 1, inc in next st] 16(17:18) times, rib to end. 58(61:64) sts.
Change to 6½ mm needles and cont in patt as folls:
1st row P2(3:4), * K4, P3, K8, P3, K4 *, P10(11:12), rep from * to * once, P to end.
2nd row K2(3:4), * P4, K3, P8, K3, P4 *, K10(11:12), rep from * to * once, K to end.
Cont in patt as set, to match Back, inc one st at each end of the 5th and every foll 4th row, working the inc sts into reverse st st, until there are 84(87:90) sts. Cont without shaping until work measures 43 cm/17 ins from beg, ending with a wrong-side row.
Place a marker at each end of last row, then work a further 19(20:21) rows.
Cast off **loosely**.

COLLAR
Join shoulder seams.
With set of four 5 mm needles and right side facing, sl first 12 sts of front neck from holder on to a spare needle, rejoin yarn, K rem 12 sts, pick up and K 21 sts evenly up right front neck, K back neck sts, pick up and K 21 sts evenly down left front neck, then K 12 sts on spare needle. 100 sts.
Working in **rows**, cont in patt as folls:
1st row (right side) K8, [P4, K4] to last 4 sts, K4.
2nd row K4, [P4, K4] to end.
3rd row K4, [C4, P4] to last 8 sts, C4, K4.
4th row As 2nd row.
These 4 rows form the patt and are rep throughout. Work 8 rows.
Change to set of four 6½ mm needles and work a further 12 rows, inc one st in centre on last row. 101 sts.
Next row K5, [P1, K1] to last 4 sts, K4.
Next row K4, [P1, K1] to last 5 sts, P1, K4.
Cast of **loosely** as set.

TO MAKE UP
Press work lightly according to instructions on ball band.
Sew in sleeves, sewing rows above markers to the cast off sts at underarms. Join side and sleeve seams.
Press seams.

RED
SUMMER
SIZZLER

Materials
11(12:13) 50 g balls of *Pingouin Cotton Naturel 8 fils*.
1 pair each of 3¼ mm (No. 10) and 4 mm (No. 8) knitting needles.

Measurements
Bust	86(91:97) cm	34(36:38) ins
Length	56(58:60) cm	22(22¾:23½) ins

Tension 24 sts and 20 rows to 10 cm over patt on 4 mm needles.

Abbreviations Alt-alternate; beg-beginning; cm-centimetres; cont-continue; foll-following; ins-inches; inc-increase; K-knit; patt-pattern; P-purl; rem-remain; rep-repeat; sl-slip; st(s):stitch(es); tog-together.

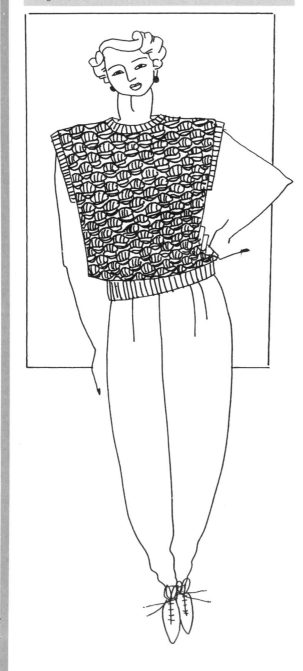

BACK
With 3¼ mm needles cast on 115(121:127) sts.
1st row (right side) K1, [P1, K1] to end.
2nd row P1, [K1, P1] to end.
Rep the last 2 rows until work measures 8 cm/3¼ ins from beg, ending with a 1st row.
Next row Rib 5(2:4), inc in next st, [rib 7(8:8), inc in next st] 13 times, rib to end. 129(135:141) sts.
Change to 4 mm needles and cont in patt as folls:
1st row K to end.
2nd row P2, [P5 winding yarn twice round needle for each st, P1] to last st, P1.
3rd row K2, [sl next 5 sts to right hand needle dropping the extra loops, sl sts back to left hand needle, and (K them tog, P them tog) twice, K them tog, winding yarn round needle twice for each st, K1] to last st, K1.
4th row P2, [K5 dropping the extra loops, P1] to last st, P1.
5th row As 1st row.
6th row P5, [P5 winding yarn twice round needle for each st, P1] to last 4 sts, P4.
7th row K4, [K1, sl next 5 sts to right hand needle dropping the extra loops, sl sts back to left hand needle, and (K them tog, P them tog) twice, K them tog, winding yarn round needle twice for each st] to last 5 sts, K5.
8th row P5, [K5 dropping the extra loops, P1] to last 4 sts, P4.
These 8 rows form the patt and are rep throughout. Cont in patt until work measures 56(58:60) cm/22(22¾:23½) ins from beg, ending with a wrong-side row.
Shape Shoulders
Cast off 43(45:47) sts at beg of next 2 rows.
Leave rem 43(45:47) sts on a holder.

FRONT
Beg with row 5 of patt, work as given for Back until Front is 16 rows less than Back to shoulders.
Shape Neck
Keeping patt correct;
Next row Patt 61(63:65), turn and leave rem sts on a spare needle.
Cast off 5 sts at beg of next row, 4 sts at beg of foll alt row, 3 sts at beg of foll alt row, 2 sts at beg of foll alt row, then one st at beg of foll 4 alt rows. 43(45:47) sts.
Cast off.
Return to the sts on spare needle; with right side facing, sl first 7(9:11) sts on to a holder, rejoin yarn, cast off 5 sts and patt to end.
Cont to match first side, reversing shaping.

NECKBAND
Join right shoulder seam.
With 3¼ mm needles and right side facing, pick up and K 27 sts evenly down left front neck, K front neck sts, pick up and K 26 sts evenly up right front neck, then K back neck sts. 103(107:111) sts.
Beg with a 2nd row, work in rib as on Back for 3 cm/1¼ ins.
Cast off **loosely** in rib.

ARMHOLE BORDERS
Join left shoulder and neckband seam.
Place markers on each side of Back and Front, 22(23:24) cm/8¾(9:9½) ins down from shoulders.
With 3¼ mm needles and right side facing, pick up and K 125(129:133) sts evenly between markers.
Beg with a 2nd row, work 1 row in rib as on Back.
Next row Rib 123(127:131), turn.
Next row Rib 121(125:129), turn.
Next row Rib 119(123:127), turn.
Next row Rib 117(121:125), turn.
Next row Rib to end.
Cast off in rib.

TO MAKE UP
Press work lightly according to instructions on ball band.
Join side seams.
Press seams.

Materials
14(15:16) 25 g balls of *Hayfield Aspen Mohair* in main colour M.
1 (1:2) balls in 1st contrast colour A.
2 (2:3) balls in 2nd contrast colour B.
1 (1:1) balls each in 3rd and 4th contrast colours C and D.
1 pair each of 5 mm (No. 6) and 5½ mm (No. 5) knitting needles.
5 buttons.

Measurements
Bust	86(91:97) cm	34(36:38) ins
Length	60 cm	23½ ins
Sleeve Seam	37 cm	14½ ins

Tension 17 sts and 19 rows to 10 cm over patt on 5½ mm needles.

Abbreviations Beg-beginning; cm-centimetres; cont-continue; dec-decrease; foll-following; ins-inches; inc-increase; K-knit; patt-pattern; P-purl; rem-remain; rep-repeat; sl-slip; st(s)-stitch(es); st st-stocking stitch.

Note When working in patt, strand yarn not in use loosely across wrong side of work.

PATTERN I (4 sts + 1)
1st row K 1A, [3M, 1A] to end.
2nd row P 1M, [1A, 1M] to end.
3rd row K [2M, 1A, 1M] to last st, 1M.
4th row As 2nd row.
5th row As 1st row.
These 5 rows complete patt I.

PATTERN II (8 sts + 1)
1st row K 1C, [3M, 1C] to end.
2nd row P [3M, 3B, 2M] to last st, 1M.
3rd row K [2M, 2B, 1M, 2B, 1M] to last st, 1M.
4th row P [1M, 2D, 3M, 2D] to last st, 1M.
5th row K [2D, 2B, 1D, 2B, 1D] to last st, 1D.
6th row As 4th row.
7th row As 3rd row.
8th row As 2nd row.
9th row As 1st row.
These 9 rows complete patt II.

PATTERN III (4 sts + 1)
1st row K 1B, [3M, 1B] to end.
Beg with a P row, work 5 rows in st st.
These 6 rows form the rep of patt.

BACK
With 5 mm needles and M, cast on 89(93:97) sts.
1st row K1, [P1, K1] to end.
2nd row P1, [K1, P1] to end.
Rep the last 2 rows once more.
Change to 5½ mm needles. Beg with a K row and working in st st throughout, work 4 rows.
Cont in patt as folls:
1st row K0(2:0) M, work 89(89:97) sts as 1st row of patt I, K0(2:0) M.
2nd row Work as given for 2nd row of patt I.
3rd row K0(1:0) A, 0(1:0) M, work 89(89:97) sts as 3rd row of patt I, K0(1:0) M, 0(1:0) A.
This sets position of patt I, work 2 more rows of patt working end sts on 2nd size as before.
With M only work 5 rows.
**11th row K0(2:0) M, work 89(89:97) sts as 1st row of patt II, K0(2:0) M.

12th row P0(0:2) B, 0(2:2) M, work 89 sts as 2nd row of patt II, P0(2:2) M, 0(0:2) B.
13th row K0(0:1) M, 0(1:2) B, 0(1:1) M, work 89 sts as 3rd row of patt II, K0(1:1) M, 0(1:2) B, 0(0:1) M.
14th row P0(0:2) M, 0(2:2) D, work 89 sts as 4th row of patt II, P0(2:2) M, 0(0:2) M.
15th row K0(0:1) D, 0(1:2) B, 0(1:1) D, work 89 sts as 5th row of patt II, K0(1:1) D, 0(1:2) B, 0(0:1) D.
This sets position of patt II, work 4 more rows of patt working end sts into patt as before.
With M only work 5 rows. ******
Work 60 rows in patt III.
Rep from ****** to ****** once, then work the 5 rows of patt I working end sts on 2nd size as before.
With M only work 5 rows.

Shape Shoulders
Cast off 15(16:17) sts at beg of next 4 rows.
Leave rem 29 sts on a holder.

LEFT FRONT
With 5 mm needles and M, cast on 43(45:47) sts and work 4 rows in rib as on Back.
Change to 5½ mm needles. Beg with a K row and working in st st throughout, work 4 rows.
Cont in patt as folls: *
1st row K0(2:0) M, work 41(41:45) sts as 1st row of patt I, 2M.

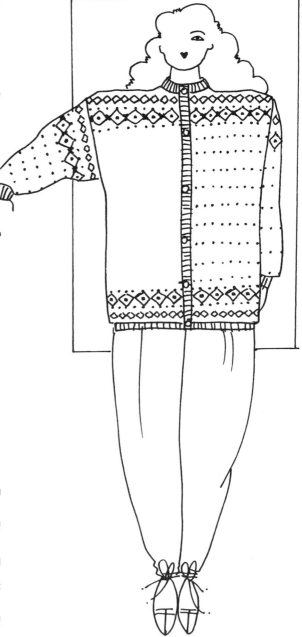

This sets position of patt I, work 4 more rows of patt working end sts into patt to match Back.
With M only work 5 rows.
11th row K0(2:0) M, work 41(41:45) sts as 1st row of patt II, 2M.
12th row P0(1:0) M, 0(3:0) B, 2M, work 41(33:41) sts as 2nd row of patt II, 0(2:2) M, 0(3:2) B, 0(1:0) M.
This sets position of patt II, work 7 more rows of patt working end sts into patt.
Cont in patt as set, to match Back, until Front is 11 rows less than Back to shoulders, thus ending with a K row.
Shape Neck
Keeping patt correct, cast off 3 sts at beg of next row.
Dec one st at end of next row and at this same edge on every foll row until 30(32:34) sts rem.
Cast off 15(16:17) sts, at beg of next row. Work 1 row, then cast off rem 15(16:17) sts.

RIGHT FRONT
Work as given for Left Front to *.
1st row K 2M, work 41(41:45) sts as 1st row of patt I, 0(2:0) M.
This sets position of patt I, work 4 more rows of patt working end sts into patt.
With M only work 5 rows.
11th row K 2M, work 41(41:45) sts as 1st row of patt II, 0(2:0) M.
12th row P0(1:0) M, 0(3:2) B, 0(2:2) M, work 41 (33:41) sts as 2nd row of patt II, 2M, 0(3:0) B, 0(1:0) M.
This sets position of patt II.
Cont in patt as set, to match Left Front reversing shaping.

SLEEVES
With 5 mm needles and M, cast on 41(43:45) sts and work in rib as on Back for 4 cm/1½ ins, ending with a 2nd row and inc 6 sts evenly across last row. 47(49:51) sts.
Change to 5½ mm needles. Beg with a K row and working in st st throughout, work 4 rows inc one st at each end of the 3rd row. 49(51:53) sts.
5th row K0(1:2) M, work 49 sts as 1st row of patt III, 0(1:2) M.
This sets position of patt, work 35 rows more in patt III, 9 rows of patt II taking care to centre patt, 5 rows using M only, 5 rows of patt I taking care to centre patt, then 5 rows using M only, **at the same time**, inc one st at each end of next and every foll 3rd row, working the inc sts into patt, until there are 61(71:81) sts, then each end of every foll 4th row until there are 81(85:89) sts.
Cast off **loosely**.

NECKBAND
Join shoulder seams.
With 5 mm needles, M and right side facing, pick up and K 15 sts evenly up right front neck, K back neck sts, then pick up and K 15 sts evenly down left front neck. 59 sts.
Beg with a 2nd row, work 4 rows in rib as on Back.
Cast off in rib.

RIGHT FRONT BAND
With 5 mm needles, M and right side facing, pick up and K 99 sts evenly up right front edge.
Beg with a 2nd row, work 3 rows in rib as on Back.
Next row Rib 2, [cast off 3, rib 20] 4 times, cast off 3, rib 2.
Next row Rib to end, casting on 3 sts over each 3 cast off.
Work 3 more rows.
Cast off **loosely** in rib.

LEFT FRONT BAND
Work as given for Right Front Band, omitting buttonholes.

TO MAKE UP
Do not press.
Sew in sleeves, with centre of sleeves to shoulder seams.
Join side and sleeve seams.
Sew on buttons.

STORMY SWEATER

Materials

11(12) 50 g balls of *Scheepjeswol Zermatt DK* in main colour M.
10(12) balls in first contrast colour A.
2(2) balls in second contrast colour B.
1 pair each of $3\frac{1}{4}$ mm (No. 10) and 4 mm (No. 8) knitting needles.

Measurements

Bust/Chest	86–97	34–38
	(102–112) cm	(40–44) ins
Length	70(78) cm	$27\frac{1}{2}(30\frac{3}{4})$ ins
Sleeve Seam	52 cm	$20\frac{1}{2}$ ins

Tension 24 sts and 24 rows to 10 cm over patt on 4 mm needles.

Abbreviations Alt-alternate; beg-beginning; cm-centimetres; cont-continue; dec-decrease; foll-following; ins-inches; inc-increase; K-knit; patt-pattern; P-purl; rem-remain; rep-repeat; rev-reverse; sl-slip; st(s)-stitch(es); st st-stocking stitch.

Note When working patt, strand yarn not in use loosely across wrong side of work. On 2nd and every alt rep of patt, read row 1 of chart from left to right. Due to the nature of the patt, it is only possible to give 2 sets of figures to cover 6 bust/chest sizes. The actual size of the garment is 117(134) cm/46($52\frac{3}{4}$) ins all round, by giving these figures, we hope it will help you to choose which size is more suited to your needs.

BACK

With $3\frac{1}{4}$ mm needles and M, cast on 117(135) sts.
1st row (right side) K1, [P1, K1] to end.
2nd row P1, [K1, P1] to end.
Rep the last 2 rows until work measures 7 cm/$2\frac{3}{4}$ ins from beg, ending with a 1st row.
Next row Rib 12(17), inc in next st, [rib 3, inc in next st] 23(25) times, rib to end. 141(161) sts.
Change to 4 mm needles and cont in patt from chart until 144(162) rows have been worked in patt.
Shape Neck
Keeping patt correct;
Next row Patt 60(70), cast off 21, patt to end.
Cont on last set of sts only; work one row straight.
Cast off 5(6) sts at beg of next and foll alt row, then 4(6) sts at beg of foll alt row.
Work one row, then cast off rem 46(52) sts.
Return to the sts which were left; with wrong side facing, rejoin yarns, cast off 5(6) sts and patt to end.
Cont to match first side reversing shaping.

FRONT

Work as given for Back until 94(112) rows have been worked in patt.
Shape Neck
Keeping patt correct;
Next row Patt 53(63), cast off 35, patt to end.
Cont on last set of sts only; dec one st at neck edge on the 5th and every foll 4th row 0(6) times, then on every foll 8th(6th) row until 46(52) sts rem.
Work 4 rows straight, then cast off.
Return to the sts which were left; with wrong side facing, rejoin yarns and patt to end.
Cont to match first side reversing shaping.

SLEEVES

With $3\frac{1}{4}$ mm needles and M, cast on 57(63) sts and work in rib as on Back for 8 cm/$3\frac{1}{4}$ ins, ending with a 2nd row and inc 8(14) sts evenly across last row. 65(77) sts.
Change to 4 mm needles and cont in patt from chart inc one st at each end of the 3rd and every foll alt row, working the inc sts into patt, until there are 89(101) sts,

then at each end of every foll 3rd row until there are 141(153) sts.
Work 3 rows straight, then cast off **loosely**.

COLLAR

With $3\frac{1}{4}$ mm needles and M, cast on 161(169) sts and work in rib as on Back for 15 cm/6 ins.
Cast off **loosely** in rib.

TO MAKE UP

Press work according to instructions on ball band.
Join shoulder seams. Sew in sleeves, with centre of sleeves to shoulder seams. Join side and sleeve seams. Sew cast on edge of collar to neck edge beg at right front shaping. Cross right half of collar over left at centre front and sew row ends of collar to cast off sts as in picture. Press seams.

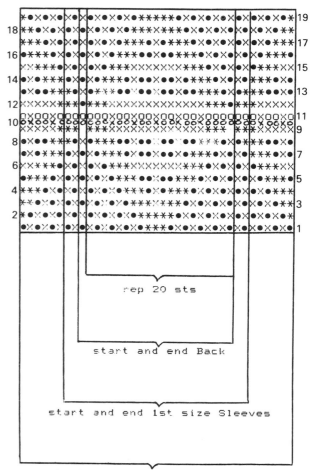

rep 20 sts

start and end Back

start and end 1st size Sleeves

start and end 2nd size Sleeves

KEY

X = st st using A
* = rev st st using A
O = st st using B
● = st st using M

A WISP OF WHITE

Materials
16(17:17) 20 g balls of *3 Suisses YSL Angora*.
1 pair each of 2¾ mm (No. 12) and 3¼ mm (No. 10) knitting needles.
1 cable needle.

Measurements
Bust	86(91:97) cm	34(36:38) ins
Length	49(51:53) cm	19¼(20:20¾) ins
Sleeve Seam	46 cm	18 ins

Tension 28 sts and 36 rows to 10 cm over patt on 3¼ mm needles.

Abbreviations Beg-beginning; cm-centimetres; cont-continue; dec-decrease; foll-following; ins-inches; inc-increase; K-knit; m 1-pick up the loop lying between the sts and work into the back of it; patt-pattern; P-purl; P1B-P1 through the back of the loop; psso-pass the slipped stitch over; rem-remain; rep-repeat; sl-slip; st(s)-stitch(es); st st-stocking stitch; tog-together; yon-yarn over needle, yrn-yarn round needle.
C8B-sl next 4 sts to cable needle to back of work, K4, then K4 from cable needle.
C8F-sl next 4 sts to cable needle to front of work, K4, then K4 from cable needle.
MB-[K1, P1, K1, P1, K1] all into next st, turn, K5, turn, P5, turn, K2 tog, K1, K2 tog, turn, K3 tog.

PATTERN PANEL A (10 sts)
1st row Yon, sl 1, K1, psso, P5, K2 tog, yrn, P1.
2nd row K2, P1, K5, P1, K1.
3rd row P1, yon, sl 1, K1, psso, P3, K2 tog, yrn, P2.
4th row K3, P1, K3, P1, K2.
5th row P2, yon, sl 1, K1, psso, P1, K2 tog, yrn, P3.
6th row K4, P1, K1, P1, K3.
7th row P3, yon, sl 1, K2 tog, psso, yrn, P3, MB.
8th row P1B, K3, P3, K3.
9th row P2, K2 tog, yrn, P1, yon, sl 1, K1, psso, P3.
10th row [K3, P1] twice, K2.
11th row P1, K2 tog, yrn, P3, yon, sl 1, K1, psso, P2.
12th row K2, P1, K5, P1, K1.
13th row K2 tog, yrn, P5, yon, sl 1, K1, psso, P1.
14th row K1, P1, K7, P1.
15th row Yrn, P3, MB, P3, yon, sl 1, K2 tog, psso.
16th row P2, K3, P1B, K3, P1.
These 16 rows form the rep of patt.

PATTERN PANEL B (20 sts)
1st row P1, K8, P2, K8, P1.
2nd and every foll alt row K1, P8, K2, P8, K1.
3rd row As 1st row.
5th row P1, C8B, P2, C8F, P1.
7th row As 1st row.
9th row As 1st row.
11th row As 1st row.
12th row As 2nd row.
These 12 rows form the rep of patt.

BACK AND FRONT (alike)
With 2¾ mm needles cast on 110(118:126) sts.
1st row (right side) K2, [P2, K2] to end.
2nd row P2, [K2, P2] to end. Rep last 2 rows until work measures 7 cm/2¾ ins from beg, ending with a 1st row.
Next row Rib 8(12:10), m 1, [rib 3, m 1] 31(31:35) times, rib to end. 142(150:162) sts.
Change to 3¼ mm needles and cont in patt as folls:
1st row P1(5:1), [work as 1st row of Panel A] 6(6:7) times, work as 1st row of Panel B, P1, [work as 1st row of Panel A] 6(6:7) times, P0(4:0).
2nd row K0(4:0), [work as 2nd row of Panel A] 6(6:7) times, K1, work as 2nd row of Panel B, [work as 2nd row of Panel A] 6(6:7) times, K1(5:1).

Work 4 more rows in patt as set.
7th row P1(5:1), [work as 7th row of Panel A] 5(5:6) times, P3, yfwd, sl 1, K2 tog, psso, yfwd, P4, work as 7th row of Panel B, P1, [work as 7th row of Panel A] 5(5:6) times, P3, yfwd, sl 1, K2 tog, psso, yfwd, P4(8:4).
8th row K4(8:4), P3, K3, [work as 8th row of Panel A] 5(5:6) times, K1, work as 8th row of Panel B, K4, P3, K3, [work as 8th row of Panel A] 5(5:6) times, K1(5:1).
Work 6 more rows in patt as set.
15th row P0(4:0), K2 tog, [work as 15th row of Panel A] 5(5:6) times, yfwd, P3, MB, P3, yfwd, sl 1, K1, psso, work as 3rd row of Panel B, K2 tog, [work as 15th row of Panel A] 5(5:6) times, yfwd, P3, MB, P3, yfwd, sl 1, K1, psso, P0(4:0).
16th row K0(4:0), [work as 16th row of Panel A] 6(6:7) times, P1, work as 4th row of Panel B, [work as 16th row of Panel A] 6(6:7) times, P1, K0(4:0).
Cont in patt until work measures 44(46:48) cm/17¼(18:19) ins from beg, ending with a wrong-side row.
Shape Neck
Keeping patt correct;
Next row Patt 37(40:45), turn and leave rem sts on a spare needle.
Dec one st at neck edge on next 9 rows. 28(31:36) sts.
Cont without shaping until work measures 49(51:53) cm/19¼(20:20¾) ins from beg, ending with a wrong-side row.
Shape Shoulder
Cast off 14(15:18) sts at beg of next row. Work one row, then cast off rem 14(16:18) sts.
Return to the sts on spare needle; with right side facing, sl first 68(70:72) sts on to a holder, rejoin yarn and patt to end.
Cont to match first side, reversing shaping.

SLEEVES
With 2¾ mm needles cast on 54(54:58) sts and work in rib as on Back for 5 cm/2 ins, ending with a 1st row.
Next row Rib 4(2:6), m 1, [rib 1, m 1] 47(49:47) times, rib to end. 102(104:106) sts.
Change to 3¼ mm needles and cont in patt as folls:
1st row P1(2:3), [work as 1st row of Panel A] 4 times, work as 1st row of Panel B, P1, [work as 1st row of Panel A] 4 times, P0(1:2).
2nd row K0(1:2), [work as 2nd row of Panel A] 4 times, K1, work as 2nd row of Panel B, [work as 2nd row of Panel A] 4 times, K1(2:3).
Cont in patt as set, to match Back, inc one st at each end of the 11th and every foll 10th(9th:8th) row, working the inc sts into patt, until there are 128(134:140) sts.
Cont without shaping until work measures 46 cm/18 ins from beg, ending with a wrong-side row.
Cast off **loosely**.

NECKBAND
Join right shoulder seam.
With 2¾ mm needles and right side facing, pick up and K 18 sts evenly down left front neck, K front neck sts, pick up and K 17(19:19) sts evenly up right front neck and 18 sts down right back neck, K back neck sts, then pick up and K 17(19:19) sts evenly up left back neck. 206(214:218) sts.
Beg with a 2nd row, work 8 rows in rib as on Body.
Cast off **loosely** in rib.

TO MAKE UP
Do not press.
Join left shoulder and neckband seam. Sew in sleeves, with centre of sleeves to shoulder seams. Join side and sleeve seams.

BUTTONS AND BOWS

Materials

14(15) 25 g hanks of *Rowan DK* in main colour M.
6(7) hanks in first contrast colour A.
5(6) hanks in second contrast colour B.
1(1) hank in third contrast colour C.
1(1) hank in fourth contrast colour D.
1 pair each of 3¼ mm (No. 10) and 4 mm (No. 8) knitting needles.
8 buttons.

Measurements

Bust	81–86(91–97) cm	32–34(36–38) ins
Length	67(72) cm	26½(28¼) ins
Sleeve Seam	53 cm	20¾ ins

Tension 26 sts and 26 rows to 10 cm over patt on 4 mm needles.

> **Abbreviations** Alt-alternate; beg-beginning; cm-centimetres; cont-continue; dec-decrease; foll-following; ins-inches; inc-increase; K-knit; patt-pattern; P-purl; rem-remain; rep-repeat; sl-slip; st(s)-stitch(es); st st-stocking stitch.

Note When working in patt, strand yarn not in use loosely across wrong side of work, weaving it in only when working across 5 or more sts.

BACK

With 3¼ mm needles and M, cast on 113(125) sts.
1st row K1, [P1, K1] to end.
2nd row P1, [K1, P1] to end.

Rep the last 2 rows until work measures 7 cm/2¾ ins from beg, ending with a 1st row.
Next row Rib 2(8), inc in next st, [rib 5, inc in next st] 18 times, rib to end. 132(144) sts.
Change to 4 mm needles. Beg with a K row and working in st st throughout, cont in patt from chart until 144(156) rows have been worked in patt.
Shape Neck
Keeping patt correct;
Next row Patt 56(60),turn and leave rem sts on a spare needle.
Cast off 2 sts at beg of next and every foll alt row until 44(48) sts rem.
Cast off.
Return to the sts which were left; with right side facing, slip first 20(24) sts on to holder, rejoin yarns, cast off 2 sts and patt to end.
Cont to match first side reversing shaping.

LEFT FRONT

With 3¼ mm needles and M, cast on 61(67) sts and work in rib as on Back for 7 cm/2¾ ins, ending with a 1st row.
Next row Rib 2(5), inc in next st, [rib 3, inc in next st] 14 times, rib to end. 76(82) sts.
Change to 4 mm needles. Beg with a K row and working in st st throughout, cont as folls:
Next row K to last 10 sts, working in patt as first row of chart, turn and leave rem sts on a holder. 66(72) sts.
Cont as set until 133(145) rows have been worked in patt.
Shape Neck
Keeping patt correct, cast off 6 sts at beg of next row, 4 sts at beg of foll alt row, 3 sts at beg of foll 2 alt rows, then 2 sts at beg of foll 3(4) alt rows. 44(48) sts.
Cont until 156(168) rows have been worked in patt.
Cast off.

RIGHT FRONT

With 3¼ mm needles and M, cast on 61(67) sts and work 6 rows in rib as on Back.

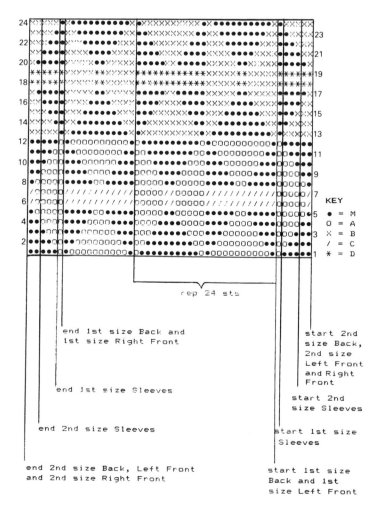

KEY
● = M
○ = A
X = B
/ = C
* = D

rep 24 sts

end 1st size Back and
1st size Right Front

start 2nd
size Back,
2nd size
Left Front
and Right
Front

end 1st size Sleeves

start 2nd
size Sleeves

end 2nd size Sleeves

start 1st size
Sleeves

end 2nd size Back, Left Front
and 2nd size Right Front

start 1st size
Back and 1st
size Left Front

Next row Rib 3, cast off 3, rib to end.

Next row Rib to end casting on 3 sts over the 3 cast off.
Cont in rib until work measures 7 cm/2¾ ins from beg,
ending with a first row.

Next row Rib 2(5), inc in next st, [rib 3, inc in next st]
14 times, rib to end. 76(82) sts.

Next row Rib 10 and sl these sts on to a holder, change
to 4 mm needles and K to end working in patt as first row
of chart.

Cont in patt as set to match Left Front, reversing shaping.

SLEEVES

With 3¼ mm needles and M, cast on 53(57) sts and work
in rib as on Back for 7 cm/2¾ ins, ending with a 2nd row
and inc 9(11) sts evenly across the last row. 62(68) sts.
Change to 4 mm needles. Beg with a K row and working
in st st throughout, cont in patt from chart, inc one st at
each end of the 3rd and every foll 4th row, working the
inc sts into patt, until there are 120(126) sts.
Work 5 rows straight, then cast off **loosely**.

BUTTON BAND

With 3¼ mm needles, M and right side facing, work in rib
across sts on holder at beg of Left Front, working twice
into the first st. 11 sts.
Cont in rib until band, when slightly stretched, reaches up
front edge, ending with a wrong-side row.
Leave sts on a holder.
Tack band in place and with pins mark the positions of
buttons; 1st to come level with buttonhole already worked,
2nd will be 1 cm from neck edge with 6 more spaced
equally between these 2.

BUTTONHOLE BAND

With 3¼ mm needles, M and wrong side facing, work in rib
across sts on holder at beg of Right Front, working twice
into the first st. 11 sts.
Cont as given for Button Band, making buttonholes as
before to correspond with positions of pins.

COLLAR

Join shoulder seams.
With right side facing, M and 3¼ mm needles, rib across
sts of Buttonhole Band, pick up and K 40 sts evenly up
right front neck and 20 sts down right back neck, K back
neck sts, dec one st in centre, pick up and K 20 sts evenly
up left back neck and 40 sts down left front neck, then rib
across sts of Button Band. 161(165) sts.
Work 8 rows in rib as set.

Next row Rib 36, turn.

Next row Rib to end.

Next row Rib 32, turn.

Next row Rib to end.

Next row Rib 28, turn.

Next row Rib to end.

Cont in this way, working 4 sts less on next and every foll
alt row until the row, rib 4, turn has been worked.

Next row Rib to end.

Next row Cast off 36 sts in rib, rib 89(93) including st on
needle after casting off, turn and leave rem sts on a spare
needle.

Next row Rib 4(6), work 3 times into next st, [rib 9,
work 3 times into next st] 8 times, rib to end. 107(111) sts.
Cont in rib until collar measures 10 cm/4 ins from beg.
Cast off **loosely** in rib.
Return to the sts on spare needle; with right side facing,
rejoin yarn and rib to end.

Next row Rib 32, turn.
Cont to match first side, reversing shaping.

TO MAKE UP

Press work lightly.
Sew in sleeves, with centre of sleeves to shoulder seams.
Join side and sleeve seams. Sew on front bands. Sew cast
off sts of shaped edge at each side of collar to row ends
on centre part of collar for about 4 cm/1½ ins, to form
lapels as in picture.
Press seams.
Sew on buttons.

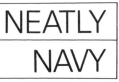

NEATLY NAVY

Materials
12(12:13) 50 g balls of *Sunbeam Pure New Wool* in main colour M.
1(1:1) ball in each of 5 contrast colours A, B, C, D and E.
1 pair each of 3¼ mm (No. 10) and 4 mm (No. 8) knitting needles.
1 cable needle.

Measurements
Bust	86(91:97) cm	34(36:38) ins
Length	73 cm	28¾ ins

Tension 34 sts and 32 rows to 10 cm over cable patt on 4 mm needles.

> **Abbreviations** Alt-alternate; beg-beginning; cm-centimetres; cont-continue; dec-decrease; foll-following; ins-inches; inc-increase; K-knit; m 1-pick up loop lying between sts and work into the back of it; patt-pattern; P-purl; rem-remain; rep-repeat; sl-slip; st(s)-stitch(es); st st-stocking stitch; tog-together.
> T6-sl next 4 sts to cable needle to front of work, K2, sl the 2 P sts from cable needle back on to left hand needle, pass the cable needle to the back of work, P2, then K2 from cable needle.

Note When working Fair Isle patt, strand yarn not in use loosely across wrong side of work.

BACK
With 3¼ mm needles and M, cast on 171(177:183) sts.
1st row (right side) K1, [P1, K1] to end.
2nd row P1, [K1, P1] to end.
Rep the last 2 rows until work measures 8 cm/3¼ ins from beg, ending with a 2nd row and inc 1(3:5) sts evenly across the last row. 172(180:188) sts.
Change to 4 mm needles and cont in patt as folls:
1st row P11(15:19), [K2, P2, K2, P6] 13 times, P to end.
2nd row K11(15:19), [P2, K2, P2, K6] 13 times, K to end.
3rd row P11(15:19), [T6, P6] 13 times, P to end.
4th row As 2nd row.
Rep the 1st and 2nd rows 3 times more.
These 10 rows form the patt and are rep throughout. Cont in patt until work measures 50(49:48) cm/19¾(19¼:19) ins from beg, ending with a wrong-side row.
Shape Armholes
Keeping patt correct, cast off 6(8:10) sts at beg of next 2 rows. 160(164:168) sts. Cont without shaping until 144 rows have been worked in patt.
Next row K13(15:17), [K2 tog, K10] 12 times, K to end. 148(152:156) sts.
Next row P to end.
** **1st row** K13(15:17) M, [1A, 4M, 2A, 4M] 11 times, 1A, 13(15:17) M.
2nd row P13(15:17) M, [1B, 3M, 4B, 3M] 11 times, 1B, 13(15:17) M.
3rd row K13(15:17) M, [1B, 2M, (2B, 2M) twice] 11 times, 1B, 13(15:17) M.
4th row P12(14:16) M, [3C, 2E, 4C, 2E] 11 times, 3C, 12(14:16) M.
5th row K12(14:16) M, [1D, 1C, (2D, 2C) twice, 1D] 11 times, 1D, 1C, 1D, 12(14:16) M.
6th row As 4th row.
7th row As 3rd row.
8th row As 2nd row.
9th row As 1st row. **
With M only and beg with a P row, work 5 rows in st st.
Rep from ** to ** once. Break off A, B, C, D and E.
With M only and beg with a P row, work 4 rows in st st.
Next row P13(15:17), m 1, [P11, m 1] 11 times, P to end. 160(164:168) sts. ***
Next row P5(7:9), [K2, P2, K2, P6] 12 times, K2, P2, K2, P to end.

Next row K5(7:9), [P2, K2, P2, K6] 12 times, P2, K2, P2, K to end.
Cont in cable patt as set, until work measures 73 cm/28¾ ins from beg, ending with a wrong-side row.
Shape Shoulders
Cast off 23(24:25) sts at beg of next 4 rows.
Leave rem 68 sts on a holder.

FRONT
Work as given for Back until 14 rows have been worked in patt.
Next row Patt 32(36:40), K11, K2 tog, K10, K2 tog, K11, turn and leave rem sts on a spare needle.
* **Next row** P34, turn and leave rem sts on a thread.
1st row K 8M, [2A, 6M] 3 times, 2M.
2nd row P 7M, [4B, 4M] 3 times, 3M.
3rd row K 6M, [2B, 2M] 6 times, 4M.
4th row P 5M, [2E, 4C, 2E] 3 times, 5M.
5th row K 5M, [1D, 2C, 2D, 2C, 1D] 3 times, 5M.
6th row As 4th row.
7th row As 3rd row.
8th row As 2nd row.
9th row As 1st row.
10th row With M, P to end.
Next row K11, m 1, K6, m 1, K6, m 1, K to end. 37 sts.
Work 3 rows in rib as on Back, then cast off in rib. *
Return to the sts on spare needle; with right side facing, rejoin M and cast on 36 sts, work in cable patt across these 36, then patt next 36 sts on spare needle, K11, K2 tog, K10, K2 tog, K11, turn and leave rem sts on spare needle.
Work from * to * once.
Return to the sts on spare needle; with right side facing rejoin M, cast on 36 sts, and patt to end.
Cont to match Back to ***, working across all sts. 172(180:188) sts.
Shape Neck
Keeping patt correct to match Back;
Next row Patt 60(62:64), turn and leave rem sts on a spare needle.
Next row Cast off 2 sts, patt to end.
Dec one st at end of next and every foll alt row until 46(48:50) sts rem.
Cont without shaping until armhole measures the same as on Back, ending with a wrong-side row.
Shape Shoulder
Cast off 23(24:25) sts at beg of next row. Work one row, then cast off rem 23(24:25) sts.
Return to the sts on spare needle; with right side facing, sl first 40 sts on to a holder, rejoin yarn, cast off 2 sts and patt to end.
Cont to match first side reversing shaping.

NECKBAND
Join right shoulder seam.
With 3¼ mm needles, M and right side facing, pick up and K 31 sts evenly down left front neck, K front neck sts, pick up and K 30 sts evenly up right front neck, then K back neck sts. 169 sts.
Beg with a 2nd row, work in rib as on Back for 6 cm/2¼ ins.
Cast off **loosely** in rib.

ARMHOLE BORDERS
Join left shoulder and neckband seam.
With 3¼ mm needles, M and right side facing, pick up and K 117(123:129) sts evenly round armhole.
Beg with a 2nd row, work in rib as on Back for 3 cm/1¼ ins.
Cast off in rib.

POCKET LININGS (make 2)
With 4 mm needles, M and right side facing, pick up and K 32 sts evenly along cast on edge at back of pocket opening.
Beg with a K row, work 14 rows in st st.
Cast off.

TO MAKE UP
Press work lightly according to instructions on ball band.
Join side seams. Fold neckband in half to inside and sl st.
Sew down pocket tops and pocket linings.
Press seams.

STEPPING SIDEWAYS

Materials

11(12) 50 g balls of *Hayfield Grampian DK*.
1 pair each of 3¼ mm (No. 10), 3¾ mm (No. 9) and 4 mm (No. 8) knitting needles.
4 mm circular needle 100 cm/42 ins long.
1 cable needle.

Measurements

Bust	81–86(91–97) cm	32–34(36–38) ins
Length	57(59) cm	22½(23¼) ins
Sleeve Seam	40 cm	15¾ ins

Tension 25 sts and 32 rows to 10 cm over centre panel on 4 mm needles.
27 sts and 32 rows to 10 cm over side patt on 4 mm needles.

Abbreviations Alt-alternate; beg-beginning; cm-centimetres; cont-continue; dec-decrease; foll-following; g st-garter stitch; ins-inches; K-knit; patt-pattern; P-purl; psso-pass the slipped stitch over; rem-remain; rep-repeat; sl-slip; ssk-sl first and 2nd sts on left hand needle to right hand needle knitwise, insert left hand needle into fronts of these sts and K them tog; st(s)-stitch(es); tbl-through the back of the loops; tog-together; yfwd-yarn forward; yrn-yarn round needle.

C3B-sl next st to cable needle to back of work, K2, then P1 from cable needle.

C3F-sl next 2 sts to cable needle to front of work, P1, then K2 from cable needle.

C5-sl next 3 sts to cable needle to back of work, K2, sl the P st from cable needle back on to left hand needle and P it, then K2 from cable needle.

Tw5-K into 5th st on left hand needle, then into 4th, then into 3rd, then into 2nd, then into first st, sl all 5 sts off needle tog.

Note When working in patt the number of sts vary on some rows. All sts quoted in instructions are counted as the original number and do not include any sts made by working patt.

BACK

With 3¾ mm needles cast on 58(60) sts. Work 5 rows in g st. Change to 4 mm needles and cont in patt as folls:
1st row (wrong side) K to end.
2nd row K5(6), [P3, (K1, yfwd, K1, yfwd, K1) into next st, P1, (K1, yfwd, K1, yfwd, K1) into next st, P3, K4] to last 1(2) sts, K to end.
3rd row P5(6), [K3, P5, K1, P5, K3, P4] to last 1(2) sts, P to end.
4th row K5(6), [P3, ssk, K1, K2 tog, P1, ssk, K1, K2 tog, P3, K4] to last 1(2) sts, K to end.
5th row P5(6), [K3, P3 tog, K1, P3 tog, K3, P4] to last 1(2) sts, P to end.
6th row K5(6), [P4, (K1, yfwd, K1, yfwd, K1) into next st, P4, K4] to last 1(2) sts, K to end.
7th row P5(6), [K4, P5, K4, P4] to last 1(2) sts, P to end.
8th row K3(4), [C3F, P3, ssk, K1, K2 tog, P3, C3B] to last 3(4) sts, K to end.
9th row K4(5), [P2, K3, P3 tog, K3, P2, K2] to last 2(3) sts, K to end.
10th row P4(5), [C3F, P5, C3B, P2] to last 2(3) sts, P to end.
11th row K5(6), [P2, K5, P2, K4] to last 1(2) sts, K to end.
12th row P5(6), [C3F, P3, C3B, P4] to last 1(2) sts, P to end.
13th row K6(7), [P2, K3, P2, K6] to last 0(1) st, K0(1).
14th row P6(7), [C3F, P1, C3B, P6] to last 0(1) st, P0(1)
15th row K7(8), [P2, K1, P2, K8] to last 12(13) sts, P2, K1, P2, K7(8).

16th row P7(8), [C5, P8] to last 12(13) sts, C5, P7(8).
These 16 rows form the patt and are rep throughout. Cont in patt until work measures 57(59) cm/22½(23¼) ins from beg, ending with a wrong-side row.
Shape Shoulders
Cast off 11 sts at beg of next 2 rows.
Leave rem 36(38) sts on a holder.

FRONT

Work as given for Back until work measures 48(50) cm/19(19¾) ins, ending with a wrong-side row.
Shape Neck
Keeping patt correct;
Next row Patt 19, turn and leave rem sts on a spare needle.
Dec one st at beg of next row and at this same edge on every foll 3rd row until 11 sts rem.
Cont without shaping until work measures the same as Back, to shoulders, ending with a wrong-side row.
Cast off.
Return to the sts on spare needle; with right side facing, sl first 20(22) sts on to a holder, rejoin yarn and patt to end.
Cont to match first side, reversing shaping.

NECKBAND

Join right shoulder seam.
With 3¼ mm needles and right side facing, pick up and K 24 sts evenly down left front neck, K front neck sts, pick up and K 24 sts evenly up right front neck, then K back neck sts. 104(108) sts.
Work 6 rows in g st, then cast off **loosely**.

SIDE PANELS AND SLEEVES

Join left shoulder and neckband seam.
With 4 mm circular needle and right side facing, pick up and K 315(325) sts evenly along side edge of Front and Back and work 6 rows in g st.
Cont in patt as folls:
1st row K5, [P5, K5] to end.
2nd row K3, P2, [K5, P5] to last 10 sts, K5, P2, K3.
Rep the last 2 rows once more, then the 1st row again.
6th row K3, P2, [Tw5, P5] to last 10 sts, Tw5, P2, K3.
These 6 rows form the patt and are rep throughout. Cont in patt until work measures 15(17) cm/6(6¾) ins, from where sts were picked up, ending with a wrong-side row.
Shape Sleeves
Keeping patt correct, cast off 80 sts at beg of next 2 rows. 155(165) sts.
Dec one st at each end of the next and every foll 4th row until 121(131) sts rem, ending with a wrong-side row.
Work 6 rows in g st.
Next row P2 tog, P2, [sl 1, K2, psso the 2 K sts, P2] to last 2 sts, P2 tog tbl.
Next row K3, [P1, yrn, P1, K2] to last st, K1.
Next row P3, [K3, P2] to last st, P1.
Next row K3, [P3, K2] to last st, K1.
Cont in patt as set dec one st at each end of the next and every foll 4th row until 99(103) sts rem, ending with a wrong-side row. Change to 3¾ mm needles.
Work 6 rows in g st, then cast off.
Work second side and sleeve in the same way.

TO MAKE UP

Press work lightly according to instructions on ball band.
Join side and sleeve seams.
Press seams.

BEATING THE BLUES

Materials
14(15:16) 50 g balls of *Pingouin Cotton Naturel* 8 fils.
1 pair each of 3¼ mm (No. 10) and 4 mm (No. 8) knitting needles.
1 cable needle.

Measurements
Bust	86(91:97) cm	34(36:38) ins
Length	52(54,56) cm	20½(21¼:22) ins
Sleeve Seam	20(21:22) cm	7¾(8¼:8¾) ins

Tension 22 sts and 40 rows to 10 cm over patt on 4 mm needles.

> **Abbreviations** Alt-alternate; beg-beginning; cm-centimetres; cont-continue; dec-decrease; foll-following; ins-inches; inc-increase; K-knit; m 1-pick up the loop lying between the sts and K into the front of it; patt-pattern; P-purl; rem-remain; rep-repeat; sl-slip; st(s)-stitch(es); tog-together.
> C8B-sl next 4 sts to cable needle to back of work, K4, then K4 from cable needle.
> C8F-sl next 4 sts to cable needle to front of work, K4, then K4 from cable needle.

BACK AND FRONT (alike)
With 3¼ mm needles cast on 106(110:118) sts.
1st row (right side) K2, [P2, K2] to end.
2nd row P2, [K2, P2] to end.
Rep the last 2 rows until work measures 8 cm/3¼ ins from beg, ending with a 1st row.
Next row Rib 10(8:6), inc in next st, [rib 3(3:4), inc in next st] 21(23:21) times, rib to end. 128(134:140) sts.
Change to 4 mm needles and cont in patt as folls:
1st row K54(57:60), P2, K4, P3, K2, P3, K4, P2, K to end.
2nd row P54(57:60), K2, P4, K3, P2, K3, P4, K2, P to end.
3rd row K1(2:1), [K2 tog] 26(27:29) times, K1, P2, K4, P3, K2, P3, K4, P2, K1, [K2 tog] 26(27:29) times, K to end.
4th row K2(3:2), [m 1, K1] 26(27:29) times, K2, P4, K3, P2, K3, P4, K3, [m 1, K1] 26(27:29) times, K1(2:1).
Rep the last 4 rows once more, then 1st and 2nd rows again.

11th row K1(2:1), [K2 tog] 26(27:29) times, K1, P2, C8F, C8B, P2, K1, [K2 tog] 26(27:29) times, K to end.
12th row K2(3:2), [m 1, K1] 26(27:29) times, K2, P16, K3, [m 1, K1] 26(27:29) times, K1(2:1).
These 12 rows form the patt and are rep throughout. Cont in patt until work measures 46(48:50) cm/18(19:19¾) ins from beg, ending with a wrong-side row.

Shape Neck
Keeping patt correct;
Next row Patt 54(56:58), turn and leave rem sts on a spare needle.
Cast off 4 sts at beg of next row, 3 sts at beg of foll alt row, 2 sts at beg of foll 2 alt rows, then one st at beg of foll 7 alt rows. Work 2 rows straight.
Cast off rem 36(38:40) sts.
Return to the sts on spare needle; with right side facing, sl first 20(22:24) sts on to a holder, rejoin yarn, cast off 4 sts and patt to end.
Cont to match first side, reversing shaping.

SLEEVES
With 3¼ mm needles cast on 78(82:86) sts and work in rib as on Body for 4 cm/1½ ins, ending with a 1st row.
Next row Rib 1(3:5), inc in next st, [rib 4, inc in next st] 15 times, rib to end. 94(98:102) sts.
Change to 4 mm needles and cont in patt as folls:
1st row K37(39:41), P2, K4, P3, K2, P3, K4, P2, K to end.
2nd row P 37(39:41), K2, P4, K3, P2, K3, P4, K2, P to end.
Cont in patt as set, to match Body, inc one st at each end of the 7th and every foll 6th row, working the inc sts into patt, until there are 112(116:120) sts.
Cont without shaping until work measures 20(21:22) cm/ 7¾(8¼:8¾) ins from beg, ending with a wrong-side row.
Cast off **loosely**.

NECKBAND
Join right shoulder seam.
With 3¼ mm needles and right side facing, pick up and K 26 sts evenly down left front neck, K front neck sts, pick up and K 25 sts evenly up right front neck, and 25 sts down right back neck, K back neck sts, then pick up and K 26 sts evenly up left back neck. 142(146:150) sts.
Beg with a 2nd row, work in rib as on Body for 8 cm/3¼ ins.
Cast off **loosely** in rib.

TO MAKE UP
Press work according to instructions on ball band.
Join left shoulder and neckband seam. Sew in sleeves, with centre of sleeves to shoulder seams. Join side and sleeve seams. Fold neckband in half to the inside and sl st. Press seams.

STYLISH AND SPORTY

Materials
22(23:24) 50 g balls of *Hayfield Brig Aran*.
1 pair each of $3\frac{3}{4}$ mm (No. 9) and $4\frac{1}{2}$ mm (No. 7) knitting needles.
Set of four $3\frac{3}{4}$ mm double pointed needles.
1 cable needle.

Measurements
Bust	86(91:97) cm	34(36:38) ins
Length	61(62:63) cm	24($24\frac{1}{2}$:$24\frac{3}{4}$) ins
Sleeve Seam	46 cm	18 ins

Tension 20 sts and 32 rows to 10 cm over m st on $4\frac{1}{2}$ mm needles.

Abbreviations Alt-alternate; beg-beginning; cm-centimetres; cont-continue; dec-decrease; foll-following; ins-inches; inc-increase; K-knit; m 1-pick up the loop lying between the sts and work into the back of it; m st-moss stitch; patt-pattern; P-purl; rem-remain; rep-repeat; sl-slip; st(s)-stitch(es).
C3F-slip next 2 sts to cable needle to front of work, K1, then K2 from cable needle.
C3B-sl next st to cable needle to back of work, K2, then K1 from cable needle.
T3F-sl next 2 sts to cable needle to front of work, P1, then K2 from cable needle.
T3B-sl next st to cable needle to back of work, K2, then P1 from cable needle.
MB-[K1, P1, K1] all into next st, turn, P3, turn, K3, turn, P3, turn, K3, sl 2nd st then 3rd st on right hand needle over the first st and off the needle.

BACK
With $3\frac{3}{4}$ mm needles cast on 95(99:105) sts.
1st row (right side) K1, [P1, K1] to end.
2nd row P1, [K1, P1] to end.
Rep the last 2 rows until work measures 7 cm/$2\frac{3}{4}$ ins from beg, ending with a 2nd row and inc 10 sts evenly across the last row. 105(109:115) sts.
Change to $4\frac{1}{2}$ mm needles and cont in patt as folls:
1st row M st 19(21:24), [P5, K2, MB, K2, P5, m st 11] 3 times, m st to end.
2nd row M st 19(21:24), [K5, P5, K5, m st 11] 3 times, m st to end.
3rd row M st 19(21:24), [P5, MB, K3, MB, P5, m st 11] 3 times, m st to end.
4th row As 2nd row.
Rep the 1st and 2nd rows once more.
7th row M st 19(21:24), [P4, C3B, P1, C3F, P4, m st 11] 3 times, m st to end.
8th row M st 19(21:24), [K4, P2, m st 3, P2, K4, m st 11] 3 times, m st to end.
9th row M st 19(21:24), [P3, T3B, m st 3, T3F, P3, m st 11] 3 times, m st to end.
10th row M st 19(21:24), [K3, P2, m st 5, P2, K3, m st 11] 3 times, m st to end.
11th row M st 19(21:24), [P2, C3B, m st 5, C3F, P2, m st 11] 3 times, m st to end.
12th row M st 19(21:24), [K2, P2, m st 7, P2, K2, m st 11] 3 times, m st to end.
13th row M st 19(21:24), [P2, K2, m st 7, K2, P2, m st 11] 3 times, m st to end.
14th row As 12th row.
15th row M st 19(21:24), [P2, T3F, m st 5, T3B, P2, m st 11] 3 times, m st to end.
16th row As 10th row.
17th row M st 19(21:24), [P3, T3F, m st 3, T3B, P3, m st 11] 3 times, m st to end.
18th row As 8th row.
19th row M st 19(21:24), [P4, T3F, P1, T3B, P4, m st 11] 3 times, m st to end.
20th row As 2nd row.
These 20 rows form the patt and are rep throughout. Cont in patt until work measures 38 cm/15 ins from beg, ending with a wrong-side row.

Shape Armholes
Keeping patt correct, cast off 12(12:13) sts at beg of next 2 rows. 81(85:89) sts.
Cont without shaping until armholes measure 23(24:25) cm/9($9\frac{1}{2}$:$9\frac{3}{4}$) ins, ending with a wrong-side row.

Shape Shoulders
Cast off 7(8:9) sts at beg of next 4 rows, then 9 sts at beg of next 2 rows.
Leave rem 35 sts on a holder.

FRONT
Work as given for Back until armholes measure 17(18:19) cm/$6\frac{3}{4}$(7:$7\frac{1}{2}$) ins, ending with a wrong-side row.

Shape Neck
Keeping patt correct;
Next row Patt 31(33:35) sts, turn and leave rem sts on a spare needle. Dec one st at neck edge on next 8 rows. 23(25:27) sts.
Cont without shaping until armhole measures the same as on Back, ending with a wrong-side row.

Shape Shoulder
Cast off 7(8:9) sts at beg of next and foll alt row. Work one row, then cast off rem 9 sts.
Return to the sts on spare needle; with right side facing, sl first 19 sts on to a holder, rejoin yarn, dec one st and patt to end.
Cont to match first side, reversing shaping.

SLEEVES
With $3\frac{3}{4}$ mm needles cast on 43(45:47) sts and work in rib as on Back for 9 cm/$3\frac{1}{2}$ ins, ending with a 1st row.
Next row Rib 7, m 1, [rib 1, m 1] 29(31:33) times, rib to end. 73(77:81) sts.
Change to $4\frac{1}{2}$ mm needles and cont in patt as folls:
1st row M st 3(5:7), [P5, K2, MB, K2, P5, m st 11] twice, P5, K2, MB, K2, P5, m st to end.
2nd row M st 3(5:7), [K5, P5, K5, m st 11] twice, K5, P5, K5, m st to end.
Cont in patt as set, to match Back, inc one st at each end of the 9th and every foll 8th row, working the inc sts into m st, until there are 97(101:105) sts.
Cont without shaping until work measures 46 cm/18 ins from beg, ending with a wrong-side row.
Place a marker at each end of the last row, then work a further 19(19:20) rows.
Cast off **loosely**.

NECKBAND AND COLLAR
Join shoulder seams.
With set of four $3\frac{3}{4}$ mm needles and right side facing, sl the first 9 sts from holder at front neck on to a spare needle, K rem 10 sts, pick up and K 21 sts evenly up right front neck, K back neck sts, pick up and K 21 sts evenly down left front neck, then K sts from spare needle. 96 sts.
Work 3 cm/$1\frac{1}{4}$ ins in rounds of K1, P1 rib.
Next row Cast off one st, m st to end, turn. 95 sts.
Working in **rows**, cont in m st for a further 8 cm/$3\frac{1}{4}$ ins.
Cast off **loosely** in m st.

TO MAKE UP
Press work lightly according to instructions on ball band. Sew in sleeves, sewing the rows above markers to the cast off sts at underarms. Join side and sleeve seams. Press seams.

RIBBON SINGLET

Materials

6(7:8) 50 g balls of *Wendy Como Cotton Ribbon*.
1 pair of $4\frac{1}{2}$ mm (No. 7) knitting needles.

Measurements

Bust	86(91:97) cm	34(36:38) ins
Length	48(50:52) cm	$19(19\frac{3}{4}:20\frac{1}{2})$ ins

Tension 15 sts and 24 rows to 10 cm over patt on $4\frac{1}{2}$ mm needles.

Abbreviations Alt-alternate; beg-beginning; cm-centimetres; cont-continue; dec-decrease; foll-following; ins-inches; inc-increase; K-knit; patt-pattern; P-purl; rem-remain; rep-repeat; sl-slip; st(s)-stitch(es); tbl-through the back of the loop; tog-together.

BACK

With $4\frac{1}{2}$ mm needles cast on 75(79:83) sts.
1st row (right side) K1 tbl, [P1, K1 tbl] to end.
2nd row P1 tbl, [K1, P1 tbl] to end.
Rep the last 2 rows until work measures 3 cm/$1\frac{1}{4}$ ins from beg, ending with a 2nd row and inc 0(1:2) sts evenly across the last row. 75(80:85) sts.
Cont in patt as folls:
1st row K to end, winding yarn twice round needle for each st.
2nd row K to end, dropping the extra loops.
These 2 rows form the patt and are rep throughout.
Cont in patt until work measures 30(31:32) cm/$11\frac{3}{4}(12\frac{1}{4}:12\frac{1}{2})$ ins from beg, ending with a wrong-side row.
Shape Armholes
Keeping patt correct, cast off 4 sts at beg of next 2 rows, 3 sts at beg of next 2 rows, then 2 sts at beg of next 2 rows.
Dec one st at each end of the next and every foll alt row until 47(50:53) sts rem.
Cont without shaping until armhole measures 16(17:18) cm/$6\frac{1}{4}(6\frac{3}{4}:7)$ ins, ending with a wrong-side row.

Shape Neck

Next row Patt 13(14:15), turn and leave rem sts on a spare needle.
Cast off 2 sts at beg of next and foll alt row, then one st at beg of foll alt row.
Cast off rem 8(9:10) sts.
Return to the sts which were left; with right side facing, sl first 21(22:23) sts on to a holder, rejoin yarn cast off 2 sts and patt to end.
Cont to match first side, reversing shaping.

FRONT

Work as given for Back until 55(58:61) sts rem, ending with a wrong-side row.
Shape Neck
Next row Work 2 tog, patt 23(24:25), turn and leave rem sts on a spare needle.
Cast off 4 sts at beg of next row, 3 sts at beg of foll alt row, 2 sts at beg of foll alt row, then one st at beg of foll 4 alt rows, **at the same time**, cont to dec at armhole edge to match Back. 8(9:10) sts.
Cont without shaping until armhole measures the same as on Back, ending with a wrong-side row.
Cast off.
Return to the sts which were left; with right side facing, sl first 5(6:7) sts on to a holder, rejoin yarn cast off 4 sts and patt to end. Cont to match first side, reversing shaping.

NECKBAND

Join right shoulder seam.
With $4\frac{1}{2}$ mm needles and right side facing, pick up and K 35 sts evenly down left front neck, K front neck sts, pick up and K 34 sts evenly up right front neck and 8 sts down right back neck, K back neck sts, then pick up and K 8 sts evenly up left back neck. 111(113:115) sts.
Beg with a 2nd row, work in rib as on Back for 2 cm/$\frac{3}{4}$ in.
Cast off in rib.

ARMHOLE BORDERS

Join left shoulder and neckband seam.
With $4\frac{1}{2}$ mm needles and right side facing, pick up and K 93(97:101) sts evenly round armhole.
Beg with a 2nd row, work in rib as on Back for 2 cm/$\frac{3}{4}$ in.
Cast off in rib.

TO MAKE UP

Do not press.
Join side seams.

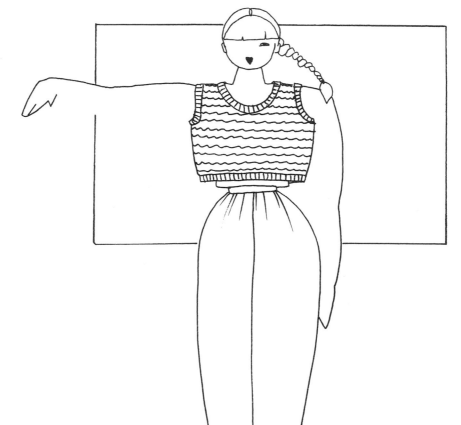

SOFT IMPRESSIONS

Materials
11(12:12) 25 g balls of *Argyll Finesse Mohair*.
1 pair each of 4½ mm (No. 7) and 5½ mm (No. 5) knitting needles.
10 buttons.

Measurements
Bust	86(91:97) cm	34(36:38) ins
Length	53(54:55) cm	20¾(21¼:21¾) ins
Sleeve Seam	44(45:46) cm	17¼(17¾:18) ins

Tension 15 sts and 22 rows to 10 cm over st st on 5½ mm needles.

> **Abbreviations** Alt-alternate; beg-beginning; cm-centimetres; cont-continue; dec-decrease; foll-following; ins-inches; inc-increase; K-knit; P-purl; rem-remain; rep-repeat; sl-slip; st(s)-stitch(es); st st-stocking stitch.

BACK
With 4½ mm needles cast on 55(59:63) sts.
1st row K1, [P1, K1] to end.
2nd row P1, [K1, P1] to end.
Rep the last 2 rows 5 times more, inc 5 sts evenly across the last row. 60(64:68) sts.
Change to 5½ mm needles and beg with a K row, cont in st st inc one st at each end of the 5th and every foll 5th row until there are 70(74:78) sts.
Cont without shaping until work measures 33 cm/13 ins from beg, ending with a P row.
Shape Armholes
Cast off 3 sts at beg of next 2 rows. 64(68:72) sts.
Dec one st at each end of the next and every foll alt row until 58(60:62) sts rem.
Cont without shaping until armholes measure 20(21:22) cm/7¾(8¼:8¾) ins, ending with a P row.
Shape Shoulders and Neck
Cast off 4 sts at beg of next 2 rows. 50(52:54) sts.
Next row Cast off 4, K16(17:18) sts including st on needle after casting off, turn and leave rem sts on a spare needle.
Next row Cast off 2, P to end.
Next row Cast off 4, K to end.
Next row Cast off 2, P to end.
Next row Cast off 3(4:4), K to end.
Next row Cast off 2, P to end.
Cast off rem 3(3:4) sts.
Return to the sts on spare needle; with right side facing, sl first 10 sts on to a holder, rejoin yarn, cast off 2 sts and K to end. Cont to match first side, reversing shaping.

LEFT FRONT
With 4½ mm needles cast on 33(35:37) sts and work 12 rows in rib as on Back, inc 3 sts evenly across the last row. 36(38:40) sts.
Change to 5½ mm needles and cont as folls:
Next row K to last 8 sts, turn and leave rem sts on a holder. 28(30:32) sts.
Beg with a P row, cont in st st inc one st at side edge on 4th and every foll 5th row until there are 33(35:37) sts.
Cont without shaping until work measures the same as Back to armholes, ending with a P row.
Shape Armhole
Cast off 3 sts at beg of next row. 30(32:34) sts.
Work one row straight.
Dec one st at beg of next row and every foll alt row until 27(28:29) sts rem.
Cont without shaping until armhole measures 14(15:16) cm/5½(6:6¼) ins, ending with a K row.
Shape Neck
Cast off 2 sts at beg of next and foll 2 alt rows, then one st at beg of foll 3 alt rows. 18(19:20) sts. Work 2 rows straight.

Shape Shoulder
Cast off 4 sts at beg of next and foll 2 alt rows, then 3(4:4) sts at beg of foll alt row.
Work one row, then cast off rem 3(3:4) sts.

RIGHT FRONT
With 4½ mm needles cast on 33(35:37) sts and work 4 rows in rib as on Back.
** **Next row** Rib 3, cast off 2, rib to end.
Next row Rib to end, casting on 2 sts over the 2 cast off. **
Work 4 rows.
Rep from ** to ** once more, inc 3 sts evenly across the last row. 36(38:40) sts. Rib 8 sts and sl these on to a holder.
Next row Change to 5½ mm needles, K to end. 28(30:32) sts.
Cont to match Left Front, reversing all shaping.

SLEEVES
With 4½ mm needles cast on 33(35:37) sts and work in rib as on Back for 5 cm/2 ins ending with a 2nd row and inc 3 sts evenly across the last row. 36(38:40) sts.
Change to 5½ mm needles and beg with a K row, cont in st st inc one st at each end of the 9th and every foll 10th row until there are 50(52:54) sts.
Cont without shaping until work measures 44(45:46) cm/17¼(17¾:18) ins from beg, ending with a P row.
Shape Top
Cast off 3 sts at beg of next 2 rows, then 2 sts at beg of next 2 rows.
Dec one st at each end of the next and every foll alt row until 26 sts rem.
Cast off 2 sts at beg of next 6 rows, then 3 sts at beg of next 2 rows.
Cast off rem 8 sts.

BUTTON BAND
With 4½ mm needles and right side facing, work in rib across sts on holder at beg of Left Front, working twice into first st. 9 sts.
Cont in rib until Band, when slightly stretched, reaches up front edge to neck, ending with a wrong-side row.
Leave sts on a holder.
Tack band in place and mark positions of buttons with pins, 1st will be on 5th row above sts on holder at neck edge, 2nd to be level with top buttonhole already worked and 7 more spaced equally between these 2.

BUTTONHOLE BAND
With 4½ mm needles and wrong side facing, work in rib across sts on holder at beg of Right Front, working twice into first st. 9 sts.
Cont to match Button Band, making buttonholes as before to correspond with positions of pins.

NECKBAND
Join shoulder seams.
With 4½ mm needles and right side facing, rib across sts of Buttonhole Band, pick up and K 18 sts evenly up right front neck and 8 sts down right back neck, K back neck sts, pick up and K 9 sts evenly up left back neck and 18 sts down left front neck, then rib across sts of Button Band. 81 sts.
Work 7 rows in rib as set, making buttonhole as before on 4th row.
Cast off in rib.

TO MAKE UP
Press work according to instructions on ball band.
Sew in sleeves. Join side and sleeve seams. Sew on front bands.
Press seams.
Sew on buttons.

COOL COTTON

Materials

19(20:21) 50 g balls of *Berger du Nord Cotton No. 5*.
1 pair each of $3\frac{3}{4}$ mm (No. 9) and $4\frac{1}{2}$ mm (No. 7) knitting needles.
Set of four $3\frac{3}{4}$ mm double pointed needles.

Measurements

Bust	86(91:97) cm	34(36:38) ins
Length	68(70:72) cm	$26\frac{3}{4}(27\frac{1}{2}:28\frac{1}{4})$ ins
Sleeve Seam	35(36:37) cm	$13\frac{3}{4}(14\frac{1}{4}:14\frac{1}{2})$ ins

Tension 19 sts and 26 rows to 10 cm over patt on $4\frac{1}{2}$ mm needles.

Abbreviations Alt-alternate; beg-beginning; cm-centimetres; cont-continue; dec-decrease; foll-following; ins-inches; inc-increase; K-knit; patt-pattern; P-purl; psso-pass the slipped stitch over; rem-remain; rep-repeat; sl-slip; st(s)-stitch(es); tbl-through the back of the loop; tog-together.
M3-[K1 tbl, K1] in next st, insert left hand needle behind vertical strand and K it tbl.
Tw2K-K 2nd st on left hand needle tbl, then K first st and sl both sts off needle tog.
Tw2P-P 2nd st on left hand needle, then P first st and sl both sts off needle tog.

BACK

With $3\frac{3}{4}$ mm needles cast on 97(103:109) sts.
1st row (right side) P1, [Tw2K, P1] to end.
2nd row K1, [Tw2P, K1] to end.
Rep the last 2 rows 3 times more, inc 4(6:8) sts evenly across the last row. 101(109:117) sts.
Change to $4\frac{1}{2}$ mm needles and cont in patt as folls:
1st row K1, [K3, P1] to last 4 sts, K4.
2nd row K1, P3, [K5, P3] to last st, K1.
Rep the last 2 rows, 4 times more.
11th row K1, sl 1, K2, psso the 2 K sts, [K2, M3, K2, sl 1,

K2 tog, psso] to last 9 sts, K2, M3, K2, sl 1, K2, psso the 2 K sts, K1.
12th row K4, [K1, P3, K4] to last st, K1.
13th row K1, [K3, P1] to last 4 sts, K4.
Rep the last 2 rows 4 times more, then the 12th row again.
23rd row K2, [K1, P1] in next st, K2, [sl 1, K2 tog, psso, K2, M3, K2] to last 8 sts, sl 1, K2 tog, psso, K2, [K1, P1] in next st, K2.
24th row As 2nd row.
These 24 rows form the patt and are rep throughout.
Cont in patt until work measures 68(70:72) cm/$26\frac{3}{4}(27\frac{1}{2}:28\frac{1}{4})$ ins from beg, ending with a wrong-side row.

Shape Shoulders

Cast off 33(36:39) sts at beg of next 2 rows.
Leave rem 35(37:39) sts on a holder.

FRONT

Work as given for Back until work measures 53(55:57) cm/$20\frac{3}{4}(21\frac{3}{4}:22\frac{1}{2})$ ins from beg, ending with a right-side row.

Divide for Front Opening

Keeping patt correct;
Next row Patt 48(52:56), cast off 5, patt to end.
Cont on last set of sts only, without shaping, until work measures 62(64:66) cm/$24\frac{1}{2}(25\frac{1}{4}:26)$ ins from beg, ending with a right-side row.

Shape Neck

Keeping patt correct, cast off 5 sts at beg of next row, 4 sts at beg of foll alt row, 3 sts at beg of foll alt row, 2 sts at beg of foll alt row, then one st at beg of foll 1(2:3) alt rows. 33(36:39) sts.
Cont without shaping until work measures the same as Back to shoulders, ending with a wrong-side row.
Cast off.
Return to the sts which were left; with right side facing rejoin yarn and patt to end.
Cont to match first side, reversing shaping.

SLEEVES

With $3\frac{3}{4}$ mm needles cast on 46 sts and work 8 rows in rib as on Back, inc 23 sts evenly across the last row. 69 sts.
Change to $4\frac{1}{2}$ mm needles and cont in patt as on Back, inc one st at each end of the 5th and every foll 4th row, working the inc sts into patt, until there are 91(95:99) sts.
Cont without shaping until work measures 35(36:37) cm/$13\frac{3}{4}(14\frac{1}{4}:14\frac{1}{2})$ ins from beg, ending with a wrong-side row.
Cast off **loosely**.

NECKBAND

Join shoulder seams.
With set of four $3\frac{3}{4}$ mm needles and right side facing, pick up and K 25 sts evenly up right front neck, K back neck sts, inc 0(1:2) sts evenly across them, then pick up and K 25 sts evenly down left front neck, 85(88:91) sts.
Beg with a 2nd row, work 6 cm/$2\frac{1}{4}$ ins in rib as on Back.
Cast off in rib.

RIGHT FRONT BAND

With $3\frac{3}{4}$ mm needles and right side facing, pick up and K 25 sts evenly up right front edge, to halfway up Neckband.
Beg with a 2nd row, work 6 cm/$2\frac{1}{4}$ ins in rib as on Back.
Cast off **loosely** in rib.

LEFT FRONT BAND

With $3\frac{3}{4}$ mm needles and right side facing, pick up and K 25 sts evenly down left front edge, beg halfway down Neckband.
Beg with a 2nd row, work 6 cm/$2\frac{1}{4}$ ins in rib as on Back.
Cast off **loosely** in rib.

TO MAKE UP

Press work lightly according to instructions on ball band. Sew in sleeves, with centre of sleeves to shoulder seams. Join side and sleeve seams. Fold neckband in half to the inside and sl st. Fold front bands in half to the inside and sl st. Join row ends at top of front bands. Lap right front band over left and sew lower ends to the cast off sts at centre front.
Press seams.

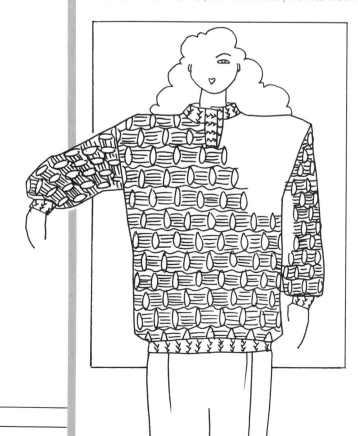

FAIR ISLE
WITH FLAIR

Measurements

Bust	86(91:97) cm	34(36:38) ins
Length	64(65:66) cm	25¼(25½:26) ins
Sleeve Seam	46 cm	18 ins

Tension 30 sts and 32 rows to 10 cm over patt on 3¼ mm needles.

Materials

4(4:5) 50 g balls of *Hayfield Grampian* 4 ply perle in main colour M.
2(3:3) balls in first contrast colour A.
2(2:3) balls in second contrast colour B.
2(2:2) balls of *Hayfield Grampian* 4 ply in third contrast colour C.
1(2:2) balls in fourth contrast colour D.
1(1:1) ball in fifth contrast colour E.
1 pair each of 2¾ mm (No. 12) amd 3¼ mm (No. 10) knitting needles.
10 buttons.

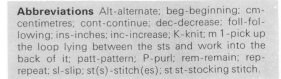

Abbreviations Alt-alternate; beg-beginning; cm-centimetres; cont-continue; dec-decrease; foll-following; ins-inches; inc-increase; K-knit; m 1-pick up the loop lying between the sts and work into the back of it; patt-pattern; P-purl; rem-remain; rep-repeat; sl-slip; st(s)-stitch(es); st st-stocking stitch.

Note When working patt, strand yarn not in use loosely across wrong side of work.

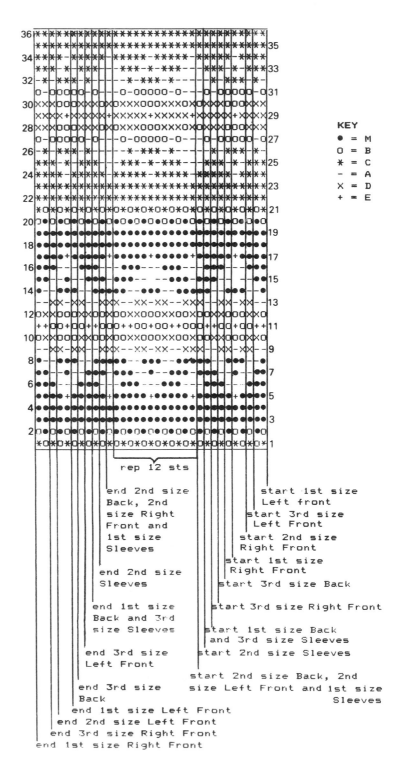

KEY

● = M
O = B
✱ = C
– = A
X = D
+ = E

BACK

With 2¾ mm needles and M, cast on 131 (139:147) sts.

1st row K1, [P1, K1] to end.

2nd row P1, [K1, P1] to end.

Rep the last 2 rows until work measures 6 cm/2¼ ins from beg, ending with a 1st row.

Next row Rib 7(12:1), m 1, [rib 4(4:5), m 1] 29 times, rib to end. 161 (169:177) sts.

Change to 3¼ mm needles. Beg with a K row and working in st st throughout, cont in patt from chart until work measures 43 cm/17 ins from beg, ending with a P row.

Shape Armholes

Keeping patt correct, cast off 7(8:9) sts at beg of next 2 rows.

Dec one st at each end of every row until 107(111:115) sts rem.

Cont without shaping until armholes measure 21 (22:23) cm/8¼(8¾:9) ins, ending with a P row.

Shape Shoulders

Cast off 10 sts at beg of next 4 rows, then 10(12:14) sts at beg of next 2 rows.

Leave rem 47 sts on a holder.

POCKET LININGS (make 2)

With 3¼ mm needles and M, cast on 33 sts and beg with a K row cont in st st until work measures 11 cm/4¼ ins from beg, ending with a P row.

Leave sts on a holder.

LEFT FRONT

With 2¾ mm needles and M, cast on 61 (65:69) sts and work in rib as on Back for 6 cm/2¼ ins, ending with a 1st row.

Next row Rib 2(4:6), m 1, [rib 4, m 1] 14 times, rib to end. 76(80:84) sts.

Change to 3¼ mm needles. Beg with a K row and working in st st throughout, cont in patt from chart until work measures 17 cm/6¾ ins from beg, ending with a P row.

Place Pocket

Next row Patt 22(24:26), sl next 33 sts on to a holder, with right side facing, patt across sts of one pocket lining, patt to end.

Cont in patt until work measures the same as Back to armholes, ending with a P row.

Shape Armhole

Keeping patt correct, cast off 7(8:9) sts at beg of next row.

Next row Patt to end.

Dec one st at beg of next row and at this same edge on every foll row until 49(51:53) sts rem.

Cont without shaping until armhole measures 15(16:17) cm/6(6¼:6¾) ins, ending with a P row.

Shape Neck

Keeping patt correct;

Next row Patt to last 10 sts, turn and leave rem sts on a holder.

Dec one st at beg of next row and at this same edge on every foll row until 30(32:34) sts rem.

Cont without shaping until armhole measures the same as on Back, ending with a P row.

Shape Shoulder

Cast off 10 sts at beg of next and foll alt row. Work one row, then cast off rem 10(12:14) sts.

RIGHT FRONT

Work as given for Left Front reversing all shaping, positions of pocket and patt.

SLEEVES

With 2¾ mm needles and M, cast on 63(65:67) sts and work in rib as on Back for 5 cm/2 ins, ending with a 1st row.

Next row Rib 10(1:2), m 1, [rib 2(3:3), m 1] 21 times, rib to end. 85(87:89) sts.

Change to 3¼ mm needles. Beg with a K row and working in st st throughout, starting with row 25, cont in patt from chart inc one st at each end of the 5th and every foll 4th row, working the inc sts into patt, until there are 131 (135:139) sts.

Cont without shaping until work measures approximately 46 cm/18 ins from beg, ending with a same patt row as on Back at armholes.

Shape Top

Keeping patt correct, cast off 7(8:9) sts at beg of next 2 rows.

Dec one st at each end of next and foll 4(5:6) alt rows, then at each end of every row until 39 sts rem.

Cast off.

BUTTON BAND

With 2¾ mm needles and M, cast on 11 sts.

1st row K1, [P1, K1] to end.

2nd row K1, [K1, P1] to last 2 sts, K2.

Rep the last 2 rows until work, when slightly stretched, reaches up left front edge, ending with a wrong-side row. Leave sts on a holder.

Tack band in place and with pins mark the positions of buttons; 1st to come 2 cm/¾ in from lower edge, 2nd will be in neckband 1 cm/½ in above sts on holder, with 8 more spaced evenly between these 2.

BUTTONHOLE BAND

Work to match Button Band, working buttonholes to correspond with position of pins as folls:

(right side) Rib 5, cast off 2, rib to end.

Next row Rib to end, casting on 2 sts over the 2 cast off.

NECKBAND

Join shoulder seams.

With 2¾ mm needles, M and right side facing, rib across sts of Buttonhole Band, K front neck sts from holder, pick up and K 19 sts evenly up right front neck, K back neck sts inc 2 sts evenly across them, pick up and K 19 sts evenly down left front neck, K front neck sts from holder, then rib across sts of Button Band. 129 sts.

Beg with a 2nd row, work 3 cm/1¼ ins in rib as set, working buttonhole as before.

Cast off in rib.

POCKET TOPS

With 2¾ mm needles, M and right side facing, K across sts on holder inc 2 sts evenly across them. 35 sts.

Work 8 rows in rib as on Back.

Cast off **loosely** in rib.

TO MAKE UP

Press work according to instructions on ball band.

Sew in sleeves. Join side and sleeve seams. Sew on front bands. Sew down pocket tops and pocket linings.

Press seams.

Sew on buttons.

A CLASSIC IN CREAM

Materials
10(10:11) 50 g balls of *Patons Clansman DK*.
1 pair each of $3\frac{1}{4}$ mm (No. 10) and 4 mm (No. 8) knitting needles.
1 cable needle.

Measurements

Bust	86(91:97) cm	34(36:38) ins
Length	60(62:64) cm	$23\frac{1}{2}(24\frac{1}{2}:25\frac{1}{4})$ ins

Tension 24 sts and 32 rows to 10 cm over st st on 4 mm needles.

Abbreviations Alt-alternate; cm-centimetres; cont-continue; dec-decrease; foll-following; ins-inches; inc-increase; K-knit; m 1-pick up the loop lying between the sts and work into the back of it; m st-moss stitch; patt-pattern; P-purl; rem-remain; rep-repeat; sl-slip; st(s)-stitch(es), st st-stocking stitch.
C4-slip next 2 sts to cable needle to front of work, K2, then K2 from cable needle.
C3F-sl next 2 sts to cable needle to front of work, K1, then K2 from cable needle.
C3B-sl next st to cable needle to back of work, K2, then K1 from cable needle.
T3F-sl next 2 sts to cable needle to front of work, P1, then K2 from cable needle.
T3B-sl next st to cable needle to back of work, K2, then P1 from cable needle.
MB-[K1, (P1, K1) 3 times] all into next st, then with point of left hand needle, pass 2nd, 3rd, 4th, 5th, 6th and 7th sts on right hand needle over the first st and off the needle.

BACK
With $3\frac{1}{4}$ mm needles cast on 91(97:103) sts.
1st row (right side) K1, [P1, K1] to end.
2nd row P1, [K1, P1] to end.
Rep the last 2 rows until work measures 5(6:7) cm/ $2(2\frac{1}{4}:2\frac{3}{4})$ ins from beg, ending with a 2nd row.
Next row Rib 1(4:7), m 1, [rib 1, m 1] 3 times, [rib 2, m 1, rib 1, m 1] 27 times, rib 2, [m 1, rib 1] 3 times, m 1, rib to end. 153(159:165) sts.
Change to 4 mm needles and cont in patt as folls:
1st row K8(11:14), [P4, K4] 4 times, [K3, P5, K7, (P4, K4) twice] 3 times, [P4, K4] twice, K to end.
2nd row P8(11:14), [K4, P4] 4 times, [P3, K2, MB, K2, P7, (K4, P4) twice] 3 times, [K4, P4] twice, P to end.
3rd row As 1st row.
4th row P8(11:14), [C4, P4] 4 times, [P3, MB, K3, MB, P7, (C4, P4) twice] 3 times, [C4, P4] twice, P to end.
Rep the 1st and 2nd rows once more.
7th row As 1st row.
8th row P8(11:14), [C4, P4] 4 times, [P2, C3B, P1, C3F, P6, (C4, P4) twice] 3 times, [C4, P4] twice, P to end.
9th row Patt 40(43:46) as set, [K2, P2, m st 3, P2, K6, (P4, K4) twice] 3 times, patt to end as set.
10th row Patt 40(43:46), [P1, T3B, m st 3, T3F, P5, (K4, P4) twice] 3 times, patt to end.
11th row Patt 40(43:46), [K1, P2, m st 5, P2, K5, (P4, K4) twice] 3 times, patt to end.
12th row Patt 40(43:46), [C3B, m st 5, C3F, P4, (C4, P4) twice] 3 times, patt to end.
13th row Patt 40(43:46), [P2, m st 7, P2, K4, (P4, K4) twice] 3 times, patt to end.
14th row Patt 40(43:46), [K2, m st 7, K2, P4, (K4, P4) twice] 3 times, patt to end.
15th row As 13th row.
16th row Patt 40(43:46), [T3F, m st 5, T3B, P4, (C4, P4) twice] 3 times, patt to end.
17th row As 11th row.
18th row Patt 40(43:46), [P1, T3F, m st 3, T3B, P5, (K4, P4) twice] 3 times, patt to end.
19th row As 9th row.
20th row Patt 40(43:46), [P2, T3F, P1, T3B, P6, (C4, P4) twice] 3 times, patt to end.
These 20 rows form the patt and are rep throughout. Cont in patt until work measures 36(37:38) cm/$14\frac{1}{4}(14\frac{1}{2}:15)$ ins from beg, ending with a wrong-side row.

Shape Armholes
Keeping patt correct, cast off 4(5:6) sts at beg of next 2 rows. 145(149:153) sts.
Cont without shaping until armholes measure 24(25:26) cm/$9\frac{1}{2}(9\frac{3}{4}:10\frac{1}{4})$ ins, ending with a wrong-side row.

Shape Shoulders
Cast off 16(17:18) sts at beg of next 4 rows, then 17 sts at beg of next 2 rows.
Leave rem 47 sts on a holder.

FRONT
Work as given for Back until armholes measure 16(17:18) cm/$6\frac{1}{4}(6\frac{3}{4}:7)$ ins, ending with a wrong-side row.

Shape Neck
Keeping patt correct;
Next row Patt 60(62:64) sts, turn and leave rem sts on a spare needle. Dec one st at beg of next and every foll alt row until 49(51:53) sts rem.
Cont without shaping until armhole measures the same as on Back, ending with a wrong-side row.

Shape Shoulder
Cast off 16(17:18) sts at beg of next and foll alt row. Work one row, then cast off rem 17 sts.
Return to the sts on spare needle; with right side facing, sl first 25 sts on to a holder, rejoin yarn and patt to end.
Cont to match first side, reversing shaping.

NECKBAND
Join right shoulder seam.
With $3\frac{1}{4}$ mm needles and right side facing, pick up and K 24 sts evenly down left front neck, K front neck sts, pick up and K 23 sts evenly up right front neck, then K back neck sts. 119 sts.
Beg with a 2nd row, work in rib as on Back for 6 cm/$2\frac{1}{4}$ ins.
Cast off **loosely** in rib.

ARMHOLE BORDERS
Join left shoulder and neckband seam.
With $3\frac{1}{4}$ mm needles and right side facing, pick up and K 139(145:151) sts evenly along armhole edge.
Beg with a 2nd row, work in rib as on Back for 3 cm/$1\frac{1}{4}$ ins.
Cast off in rib.

TO MAKE UP
Press work lightly according to instructions on ball band.
Join side seams. Fold neckband in half to the inside and sl st.
Press seams.

TASTEFULLY TEXTURED

Materials
18(19:20) 50 g balls of *W. H. Smith Pure English Chunky Wool.*
1 pair each of 4½ mm (No. 7) and 5½ mm (No. 5) knitting needles.
Set of four 4½ mm double pointed needles.
1 cable needle.

Measurements
Bust	86(91:97) cm	34(36:38) ins
Length	56(58:60) cm	22(22¾:23½) ins
Sleeve Seam	43(44:45) cm	17(17¼:17¾) ins

Tension 22 sts and 21 rows to 10 cm over patt on 5½ mm needles.

Abbreviations Alt-alternate; beg-beginning; cm-centimetres; cont-continue; dec-decrease; foll-following; ins-inches; inc-increase; K-knit; patt-pattern; P-purl; rem-remain; rep-repeat; sl-slip; sl 1P-slip next st purlwise; st(s)-stitch(es); tog-together; yon-yarn over needle to make a stitch; yfwd-yarn forward round last st.
C6F-sl next 3 sts to cable needle to front of work, K3, then K3 from cable needle.
C6B-sl next 3 sts to cable needle to back of work, K3, then K3 from cable needle.

BACK AND FRONT (alike)
With 4½ mm needles cast on 107(112:117) sts.
1st row (wrong side) K2, [P3, K2] to end.
2nd row P2, [K1, sl 1, K1, P2] to end.
Rep the last 2 rows until work measures 7 cm/2¾ ins from beg, ending with a 2nd row.
Next row Rib 5(4:4), inc in next st, [rib 7(7:8), inc in next st] 12(13:12) times, rib to end. 120(126:130) sts.
Change to 5½ mm needles and cont in patt as folls:
1st row P1(4:6), [yon, sl 1P, yfwd, P3, C6F, P3, yon, sl 1P, yfwd, P3, C6B, P3] 4 times, yon, sl 1P, yfwd, P3, C6F, P3, yon, sl 1P, yfwd, P1(4:6).
2nd row K1(4:6), [P the yon and the sl st tog, K3, P6, K3] 9 times, P the yon and the sl st tog, K1(4:6).
3rd row P1(4:6), [yon, sl 1P, yfwd, P3, K6, P3] 9 times, yon, sl 1P, yfwd, P1(4:6).
4th row As 2nd row.
Rep the last 2 rows twice more.
9th row P1(4:6), [yon, sl 1P, yfwd, P3, C6B, P3, yon, sl 1P, yfwd, P3, C6F, P3] 4 times, yon, sl 1P, yfwd, P3, C6B, P3, yon, sl 1P, yfwd, P1(4:6).
10th row As 2nd row.
Rep the 3rd and 4th rows 3 times more.
These 16 rows form the patt and are rep throughout. Cont in patt until work measures 48(50:52) cm/19(19¾:20½) ins from beg, ending with a wrong-side row.
Shape Neck
Keeping patt correct;
Next row Patt 50(53:55), turn and leave rem sts on a spare needle. Cast off 4 sts at beg of next row, 3 sts at beg of foll alt row, then 2 sts at beg of foll alt row.
Work one row straight, then dec one st at beg of next and foll 4 alt rows.
Cast off rem 36(39:41) sts.
Return to the sts on spare needle; with right side facing, sl first 20 sts on to a holder, rejoin yarn, cast off 4 sts and patt to end.
Cont to match first side, reversing shaping.

SLEEVES
With 4½ mm needles, cast on 62 sts and work in rib as on Back for 5 cm/2 ins, ending with a 1st row and inc 6 sts evenly across the last row. 68 sts.
Change to 5½ mm needles and cont in patt as folls:
1st row P1, [yon, sl 1P, yfwd, P3, C6F, P3, yon, sl 1P,

yfwd, P3, C6B, P3] twice, yon, sl 1P, yfwd, P3, C6F, P3, yon, sl 1P, yfwd, P1.
2nd row K1, [P the yon and the sl st tog, K3, P6, K3] 5 times, P the yon and the sl st tog, K1.
Cont in patt as set, to match Body, inc one st at each end of next and every foll 4th row, working the inc sts into patt, until there are 100(104:108) sts. Cont without shaping until work measures 43(44:45) cm/17(17¼:17¾) ins from beg, ending with a wrong-side row.
Cast off **loosely.**

NECKBAND
Join shoulder seams.
With set of four 4½ mm needles and right side facing, pick up and K 17 sts down left front neck, K front neck sts, pick up and K 18 sts up right front neck and 17 sts down right back neck, K back neck sts, then pick up and K 18 sts up left back neck. 110 sts.
Next round [P2, K3] to end.
Next round [P2, K1, sl 1, K1] to end.
Rep the last 2 rounds for 5 cm/2 ins.
Cast off **loosely** in rib.

TO MAKE UP
Press work lightly according to instructions on ball band. Sew in sleeves, with centre of sleeves to shoulder seams. Join side and sleeve seams. Press seams.

DIVERTING DIAGONALS

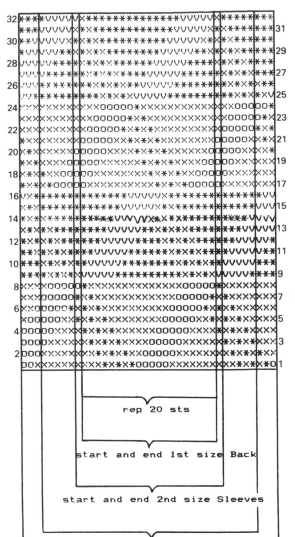

Materials
8(9) 50 g balls of *Emu Superwash DK* in main colour M.
7(8) balls of contrast colour C.
1 pair each of $3\frac{1}{4}$ mm (No. 10) and 4 mm (No. 8) knitting needles.

Measurements
Bust	81–86(91–97) cm	32–34(36–38) ins
Length	58(65) cm	$22\frac{3}{4}(25\frac{1}{2})$ ins
Sleeve Seam	52 cm	$20\frac{1}{2}$ ins

Tension 22 sts and 24 rows to 10 cm over patt on 4 mm needles.

Abbreviations Alt-alternate; beg-beginning; cm-centimetres; cont-continue; dec-decrease; foll-following; ins-inches; inc-increase; K-knit; patt-pattern; P-purl; rem-remain; rep-repeat; rev-reverse; sl-slip; st(s):stitch(es); st st-stocking stitch.

Note When working in patt, strand yarn not in use loosely across wrong side of work.

BACK
With $3\frac{1}{4}$ mm needles and M, cast on 107(113) sts.
1st row (right side) K1, [P1, K1] to end.
2nd row P1, [K1, P1] to end.
Rep the last 2 rows until work measures 5 cm/2 ins from beg, ending with a 1st row.
Next row Rib 5(2), inc in next st, [rib 7(5), inc in next st] 12(18) times, rib to end. 120(132) sts.
Change to 4 mm needles and cont in patt from chart until 120(136) rows have been worked in patt.
Shape Neck
Keeping patt correct;
Next row Patt 50(54), turn and leave rem sts on a spare needle.
Cast off 3 sts at beg of next and foll alt row, then 2 sts at beg of foll 2 alt rows.
Cast off rem 40(44) sts.
Return to the sts on spare needle; with right side facing, sl first 20(24) sts on to a holder, rejoin yarns, cast off 3 sts and patt to end.
Cont to match first side reversing shaping.

FRONT
Work as given for Back until 112(128) rows have been worked in patt.
Shape Neck
Keeping patt correct;
Next row Patt 50(54), turn and leave rem sts on a spare needle.
Cast off 3 sts at beg of next row, 2 sts at beg of foll 2 alt rows, then one st at beg of foll 3 alt rows.
Work 4 rows straight, then cast off rem 40(44) sts.
Return to the sts on spare needle; with right side facing, sl first 20(24) sts on to a holder, rejoin yarns, cast off 3 sts and patt to end.
Cont to match first side reversing shaping.

SLEEVES
With $3\frac{1}{4}$ mm needles and M, cast on 57(61) sts and work in rib as on Back for 5 cm/2 ins, ending with a 2nd row and inc one st in centre of last row. 58(62) sts.
Change to 4 mm needles and cont in patt from chart inc one st at each end of the 3rd and every foll 4th row, working the inc sts into patt, until there are 112(116) sts.
Work 5 rows, then cast off **loosely**.

NECKBAND
Join left shoulder seam.
With $3\frac{1}{4}$ mm needles, M and right side facing, pick up and K 14 sts evenly down right back neck, K back neck sts, pick up and K 13 sts evenly up left back neck and 21 sts down left front neck, K front neck sts, then pick up and K 21 sts evenly up right front neck. 109(117) sts.
Beg with a 2nd row, work in rib as on Back for 5 cm/2 ins.
Cast off **loosely** in rib.

TO MAKE UP
Press work according to instructions on ball band.
Join right shoulder and neckband seam. Sew in sleeves, with centre of sleeves to shoulder seams. Join side and sleeve seams. Fold neckband in half to the inside and sl st. Press seams.

KEY
V = rev st st with C
O = rev st st with M
X = st st with C
* = st st with M

A SAMPLER FOR SPRING

Materials
2(2:2) 450 g cones of *Rowan Mercerised Cotton*.
1 pair each of 3 mm (No. 11) and 3¾ mm (No. 9) knitting needles.

Measurements

Bust	86(91:97) cm	34(36:38) ins
Length	49(50:51) cm	19¼(19¾:20) ins
Sleeve Seam	38(39,40) cm	15(15¼,15¾) ins

Tension 26 sts and 40 rows to 10 cm over patt on 3¾ mm needles.

Abbreviations Alt-alternate; beg-beginning; cm-centimetres; cont-continue; dec-decrease; foll-following; ins-inches; inc-increase; K-knit; m st-moss stitch; P-purl; patt-pattern; rem-remain; rep-repeat; sl-slip; st(s)-stitch(es); st st-stocking stitch.

PATTERN PANEL (19 sts)
1st row K2, [P4, K1] 3 times, K2.
2nd row P2, K1, [P1, K4] twice, P1, K3, P2.
3rd row K2, P2, [K1, P4] twice, K1, P2, K2.
4th row P2, K3, [P1, K4] twice, P1, K1, P2.
5th row K2, [K1, P4] 3 times, K2.
6th row P2, [P1, K4] 3 times, P2.
7th row K2, P3, [K1, P4] twice, K1, P1, K2.
8th row P2, K2, [P1, K4] twice, P1, K2, P2.
9th row K2, P1, [K1, P4] twice, K1, P3, K2.
10th row P2, [K4, P1] 3 times, P2.
These 10 rows form the rep of patt.

BACK
With 3 mm needles cast on 123(131:139) sts.
1st row (right side) K1, [P1, K1] to end.
2nd row P1, [K1, P1] to end.
Rep the last 2 rows until work measures 5 cm/2 ins from beg, ending with a 2nd row.
Change to 3¾ mm needles and cont in patt as folls:
1st row [K1, P1] 9(11:13), K to last 18(22:26), [P1, K1] to end.
2nd row [K1, P1] 9(11:13) times, P to last 18(22:26), [P1, K1] to end.
3rd row M st 18(22:26), * work 19 sts as first row of panel, m st 15, rep from * once more, work 19 sts as first row of panel, m st to end.
4th row M st 18(22:26), * work 19 sts as 2nd row of panel, m st 15, rep from * once more, work 19 sts as 2nd row of panel, m st to end.
Work 18 more rows as set, working panel sts as above and rem sts in m st.
23rd row As 1st row.
24th row As 2nd row.
25th row M st 18(22:26), * K2, m st 15, K17, rep from * once more, K2, m st 15, K2, m st to end.
26th row M st 18(22:26), * P2, m st 15, P17, rep from * once more, P2, m st 15, P2, m st to end.
Rep the last 2 rows 9 times more.
These 44 rows form the patt, rep them twice more, then the first 24 rows again. (156 rows in patt). **
Next row K1, [P1, K1] to end.
Rep the last row until work measures 46(47:48) cm/18(18½:19) ins from beg, ending with a wrong-side row.
Shape Neck
Working in m st throughout;
Next row M st 49(53:57), turn and leave rem sts on a spare needle. Cast off 4 sts at beg of next row, 3 sts at beg of foll 2 alt rows, then 2 sts at beg of foll 2 alt rows. 35(39:43) sts.
Work 2 rows straight, then cast off.
Return to the sts on spare needle; with right side facing, sl first 25 sts on to a holder, rejoin yarn, cast off 4 sts and m st to end.
Cont to match first side reversing shaping.

FRONT
Work as given for Back to **.
Working in m st throughout to match Back, cont if necessary, until front is 20 rows less than Back to shoulders.
Shape Neck
Next row M st 49(53:57), turn and leave rem sts on a spare needle.
Cast off 2 sts at beg of next and foll 5 alt rows, then one st at beg of foll 2 alt rows. 35(39:43) sts.
Work 4 rows straight, then cast off.
Return to the sts on spare needle; with right side facing, sl first 25 sts on to a holder, rejoin yarn, cast off 2 sts and m st to end.
Cont to match first side reversing shaping.

SLEEVES
With 3 mm needles cast on 55(59:63) sts and work in rib as on Back for 5(6:7) cm/2(2¼:2¾) ins, ending with a 2nd row and inc one st in centre of last row. 56(60:64) sts.
Change to 3¾ mm needles and cont in patt as folls:
1st row K0(1:2), m st 15, K2, m st 22(24:26), K2, m st 15, K0(1:2).
2nd row P0(1:2), m st 15, P2, m st 22(24:26), P2, m st 15, P0(1:2).
3rd row Work twice into first st, patt as set to last st, work twice into last st.
4th row P1(2:3), patt to last 1(2:3) sts, P to end.
Work 2 rows as set.
7th row As 3rd row.
8th row P2(3:4), patt to last 2(3:4) sts, P to end.
Work 12 rows as set, inc one st at each end of rows 11, 15 and 19, working the inc sts into st st. 66(70:74) sts.
21st row K22(23:24), m st 22(24:26), K to end.
22nd row P22(23:24), m st 22(24:26), P to end.
23rd row Work twice into first st, m st 2(3:4), work 19 sts as first row of panel, m st 22(24:26), work 19 sts as first row of panel, m st 2(3:4), work twice into last st.
Work 19 rows as set, working the panel sts as before and inc one st at each end of rows 27, 31, 35 and 39, working the inc sts into m st. 76(80:84) sts.
43rd row Work twice into first st, K26(27:28), m st 22(24:26), K to last st, work twice into last st.
44th row P28(29:30), m st 22(24:26), P to end.
45th row K11(12:13), m st 15, K2, m st 22(24:26), K2, m st 15, K to end.
46th row P11(12:13), m st 15, P2, m st 22(24:26), P2, m st 15, P to end.
Work 18 rows as set, inc one st at each end of the next row and rows 51, 55, 59 and 63, working the inc sts into st st. 88(92:96) sts.
Cont in patt as set, keeping centre 22(24:26) sts in m st throughout and alternating side panels to match Body, **at the same time**, inc one st at each end of every foll 4th row until there are 122(126:130) sts.
Work one row, then cast off **loosely**.

NECKBAND
Join left shoulder seam.
With 3 mm needles and right side facing, pick up and K 21 sts evenly down right back neck, K back neck sts, pick up and K 20 sts evenly up left back neck and 25 sts down left front neck, K front neck sts, then pick up and K 25 sts evenly up right front neck. 141 sts.
Beg with a 2nd row, work in rib as on Back for 2 cm/¾ in.
Cast off **loosely** in rib.

TO MAKE UP
Press work lightly.
Join right shoulder and neckband seam. Sew in sleeves, with centre of sleeves to shoulder seams. Join side and sleeve seams.
Press seams.

LONG AND LANGUOROUS

Materials
8(9:9) 100 g hanks of *Naturally Beautiful Lin Silk* in main colour, M.
1 hank in contrast colour, C (**or** embroidery silk).
1 pair each of $2\frac{3}{4}$mm (No. 12) and $3\frac{1}{4}$mm (No. 10) knitting needles.
3 buttons.

Measurements

Bust	86(91:97) cm	34(36:38) ins
Length	67(69:71) cm	$26\frac{1}{2}(27\frac{1}{4}:28)$ ins
Sleeve Seam	45(46:47) cm	$17\frac{3}{4}(18:18\frac{1}{2})$ ins

Tension 36 sts and 32 rows to 10 cm over patt on $3\frac{1}{4}$mm needles.

Abbreviations Alt-alternate; beg-beginning; cm-centimetres; cont-continue; dec-decrease; foll-following; ins-inches; inc-increase; K-knit; m1-pick up loop lying between sts and work into the back of it; patt-pattern; P-purl; rem-remain; rep-repeat; sl-slip; st(s)-stitch(es).

BACK
With $2\frac{3}{4}$mm needles and C, cast on 139(147:155) sts.
** **1st row** (right side) K1, [P1, K1] to end.
Break off C and join in M.
2nd row P1, [K1, P1] to end.
Cont in rib as set, until work measures 7 cm/$2\frac{3}{4}$ins from beg, ending with a 2nd row. **
Next row Rib 12(16:1), inc in next st, [rib 2(2:3), inc in next st] 38 times, rib to end. 178(186:194) sts.
Change to $3\frac{1}{4}$mm needles and cont in patt as folls:
1st row K1, [K2, P4, K2] to last st, K1.
2nd row P1, [P2, K4, P2] to last st, P1.
Rep the last 2 rows once more, then the 1st row again.
6th row P1, [P2, K into 4th st on left hand needle, then into 3rd st, then into 2nd st, then into first st and sl all 4 sts off needle together, P2] to last st, P1.
These 6 rows form the patt and are rep throughout. Cont in patt until work measures 43(44:45) cm/$17(17\frac{1}{4}:17\frac{3}{4})$ ins from beg, ending with a wrong-side row.
Shape Armholes
Keeping patt correct, cast off 27(29:31) sts at beg of next 2 rows. 124(128:132) sts. ***
Cont without shaping until armholes measure 24(25:26) cm/$9\frac{1}{2}(9\frac{3}{4}:10\frac{1}{4})$ ins, ending with a wrong-side row.
Shape Shoulders
Cast off 18(19:20) sts at beg of next 4 rows.
Leave rem 52 sts on a holder.

FRONT
Work as given for Back to ***
Cont without shaping until armholes measure 5(6:7) cm/ $2(2\frac{1}{4}:2\frac{3}{4})$ ins, ending with a wrong-side row.
Divide for Front Opening
Next row Patt 57(59:61), cast off 10, patt to end.
Cont on last set of sts only, without shaping until arm hole measures 16(17:18) cm/$6\frac{1}{4}(6\frac{3}{4}:7)$ ins, ending with a wrong-side row.
Shape Neck
Keeping patt correct, cast off 7 sts at beg of next row.
Dec one st at neck edge on next 5 rows. Work one row straight, then dec one st at end of next and every foll alt row until 36(38:40) sts rem.
Cont without shaping until armhole measures the same as on Back, ending with a right-side row.
Shape Shoulder
Cast off 18(19:20) sts at beg of next row. Work one row, then cast off rem 18(19:20) sts.
Return to the sts which were left; with wrong side facing, rejoin yarn and patt to end.
Cont to match first side, reversing shaping.

SLEEVES
With $2\frac{3}{4}$mm needles and C, cast on 51(55:59) sts and work from ** to ** on Back.
Next row Rib 6, m 1, [rib 1, m 1] 38(42:46) times, rib to end. 90(98:106) sts.
Change to $3\frac{1}{4}$mm needles and cont in patt as on Back, inc one st at each end of the 3rd and every foll alt row 3(1:0) times, working inc sts into patt, until there are 98(102:108) sts.
Work 2 rows straight, then inc one st at each end of next and every foll 3rd row until there are 172(180:188) sts.
Cont without shaping until work measures 45(46:47) cm/ $17\frac{3}{4}(18:18\frac{1}{2})$ ins from beg, ending with a wrong-side row.
Place a marker at each end of last row, then work a further 24(26:28) rows.
Cast off **loosely**.

BUTTON BAND
With $2\frac{3}{4}$mm needles, M and right side facing, pick up and K 37 sts evenly down left front opening.
Work 8 rows in rib as on Back. Break off M and join in C.
Work one row, then cast off in rib.

BUTTONHOLE BAND
With $2\frac{3}{4}$mm needles, M and right side facing, pick up and K 37 sts evenly up right front opening.
Work 6 rows in rib as on Back.
Next row Rib 6, [cast off 4, rib 6] 3 times, rib 1.
Next row Rib to end, casting on 4 sts over each 4 cast off.
Break off M and join in C.
Work one row, then cast off in rib.

COLLAR
Join shoulder seams.
With $2\frac{3}{4}$mm needles, M and right side facing, pick up and K 30 sts evenly up right front neck, beg at pick up row for Buttonhole Band, K back neck sts inc one st in centre, then pick up and K 30 sts evenly down left front neck, ending at pick up row for Button Band. 113 sts.
With M only, work 10 rows in rib as on Back.
Next row Rib 46, [work 3 times into next st, rib 1] 10 times, work 3 times into next st, rib to end. 135 sts.
Cont in rib as set until collar measures 8 cm/$3\frac{1}{4}$ins from beg.
Break off M and join in C.
Work one row, then cast off **loosely** in rib.

TO MAKE UP
Press work lightly according to instructions on hank band.
Sew in sleeves, sewing the rows above markers to the cast off sts at underarms. Join side and sleeve seams. Sew ends of front bands to the cast off sts at centre front.
Press seams.
Sew on buttons.

NEW-WAVE NORWEGIAN

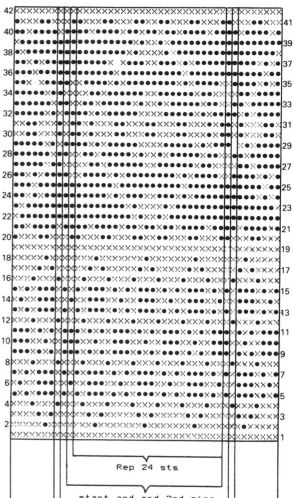

Materials
8(9) 50 g balls of *Argyll Ambridge DK* in main colour M.
6(6) balls in contrast colour C.
1 pair each of 3¼ mm (No. 10) and 4 mm (No. 8) knitting needles.

Measurements

Bust	81–86(91–97) cm	32–34(36–38) ins
Length	66(68) cm	26(26¾) ins
Sleeve Seam	45(46) cm	17¾(18) ins

Tension 26 sts and 25 rows to 10 cm over patt on 4 mm needles.

> **Abbreviations** Alt-alternate; beg-beginning; cm-centimetres; cont-continue; dec-decrease; foll-following; ins-inches; inc-increases; K-knit; m 1-pick up the loop lying between the sts and work into the back of it; patt-pattern; P-purl; rem-remain; rep-repeat; sl-slip; st(s)-stitch(es); st st-stocking stitch; tbl-through the back of loops; tog-together.

Note When working in patt, strand yarn not in use loosely across wrong side of work, weaving it only when working across 5 or more sts.

BACK
With 3¼ mm needles and M, cast on 97(103) sts.
1st row K1, [P1, K1] to end.
2nd row P1, [K1, P1] to end.
Rep the last 2 rows until work measures 8 cm/3¼ ins from beg, ending with a 1st row.
Next row Rib 7(11), m 1, [rib 2, m 1] 41 times, rib to end. 139(145) sts.
Change to 4 mm needles. Beg with a K row and working in st st throughout, cont in patt from chart until work measures 40(41) cm/15¾(16¼) ins from beg, ending with a P row.
Shape Raglans
Keeping patt correct, cast off 5 sts at beg of next 2 rows.
Dec one st at each end of next and every foll alt row until 93(97) sts rem, ending with a P row.
Dec 1 st at each end of next and every row until 41 sts rem, ending with a P row.
Leave sts on a holder.

FRONT
Work as given for Back until 77 sts rem, ending with a P row.
Shape Neck
Keeping patt correct;
Next row K2 tog, patt 28, turn and leave rem sts on a spare needle.
Next row P2 tog tbl, patt to last 2 sts, P2 tog, cont to dec at each end of every row until 9 sts rem.
Keeping neck edge straight, cont to dec at armhole edge only until 2 sts rem, ending with a P row.
K2 tog and fasten off.
Return to the sts on spare needle; with right side facing, sl first 17 sts on to a holder, rejoin yarns, patt to last 2 sts, K2 tog tbl.
Next row P2 tog tbl, patt to last 2 sts, P2 tog.
Cont to match first side, reversing shaping.

SLEEVES
With 3¼ mm needles and M, cast on 45(47) sts and work in rib as on Back for 6 cm/2¼ ins, ending with a 1st row.
Next row Rib 8(9), m 1, [rib 1, m 1] 29 times, rib to end. 75(77) sts.
Change to 4 mm needles. Starting with row 25 of chart beg with a K row and working in st st throughout, cont in patt from chart inc one st at each end of the 3rd and every foll 6th row, working the inc sts into patt, until there are 107(111) sts.

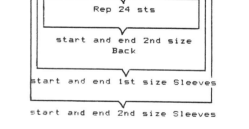

KEY
X = M
● = C

Cont without shaping until work measures approximately 45(46) cm/17¾(18) ins from beg, ending with the same patt row as on Back at armholes.
Shape Top
Keeping patt correct, cast off 5 sts at beg of next 2 rows.
Dec one st at each end of next and every foll alt row until 51 sts rem ending with a P row.
Dec one st at each end of next and every row until 19 sts rem ending with a P row.
Leave sts on a holder.

NECKBAND
Join 3 raglan seams, leaving left back raglan open.
With 3¼ mm needles, M and right side facing, K sts of left sleeve, pick up and K 18 sts evenly down left front neck, K front neck sts, pick up and K 18 sts evenly up right front neck, then K sts of right sleeve and back neck, knitting 2 tog at seam. 131 sts.
Beg with a 2nd row, work in rib as on Back for 9 cm/3½ ins.
Cast off **loosely** in rib.

TO MAKE UP
Press work according to instructions on ball band.
Join left back raglan and neckband seam. Join side and sleeve seams.
Fold neckband in half to inside and sl st.
Press seams.

SIMPLY SUMMER

Materials
2(2) 450 g cones of *Rowan Mercerised Cotton*.
1 pair each of 2¾ mm (No. 12), 3 mm (No.11) and 3¼ mm (No. 10) knitting needles.
1 cable needle.

Measurements

Bust	81–86(91–97) cm	32–34(36–38) ins
Length	50(52) cm	19¾(20½) ins

Tension 36 sts and 44 rows to 10 cm over patt I on 3¼ mm needles.
36 sts and 36 rows to 10 cm over patt II on 3¼ mm needles.

Abbreviations Alt-alternate; beg-beginning; cm-centimetres; cont-continue; dec-decrease; foll-following; ins-inches; inc-increase; K-knit; patt-pattern; P-purl; psso-pass slipped stitch over; rem-remain; rep-repeat; sl-slip; ssk-sl first and 2nd sts on left hand needle knitwise on to right hand needle, insert left hand needle into fronts of these and K them tog; st(s)-stitch(es); tog-together; yfwd-yarn forward; yrn-yarn round needle.
C6B-sl next 3 sts to cable needle to back of work, K3, then K3 from cable needle.
C6F-sl next 3 sts to cable needle to front of work, K3, then K3 from cable needle.

Note When working patt II the number of sts vary, when working shaping always count sts as the original number.

BACK
With 3 mm needles cast on 169(183) sts.
1st row (right side) K1, [P1, K1] to end.
2nd row P1, [K1, P1] to end.
Rep the last 2 rows 3 times more, then first row again.
Change to 3¼ mm needles and cont in patt as folls:
1st and every foll alt row K1, [P2 tog, yrn, P11, K1] to end.
2nd row K1, [ssk, yfwd, C6B, K6] to end.
4th row K1, [ssk, yfwd, K12] to end.
6th row K1, [ssk, yfwd, K3, C6F, K3] to end.
8th row As 4th row.
These 8 rows form patt I and are rep throughout. Cont in patt until work measures 28(29) cm/11(11½) ins from beg, ending with a wrong-side row.
Shape Armholes
Keeping patt correct, cast off 6(8) sts at beg of next 2 rows. 157(167) sts.
Work 8 rows in rib as at beg.
Cont in patt as folls:
1st row P2, [sl 1, K2, psso the 2 K sts, P2] to end.
2nd row K2, [P1, yrn, P1, K2] to end.
3rd row P2, [K3, P2] to end.
4th row K2, [P3, K2] to end.
These 4 rows form patt II and are rep throughout.
** Cont in patt until armholes measure approximately 22(23) cm/8¾(9) ins, ending with a 4th patt row.
Shape Shoulders
Cast off 25(27) sts at beg of next 2 rows, then 26(28) sts at beg of next 2 rows.
Leave rem 55(57) sts on a holder.

FRONT
Work as given for Back to **.
Cont in patt until armholes measure 14(15) cm/5½(6) ins, ending with a wrong-side row.
Shape Neck
Keeping patt correct;
Next row Patt 64(68), turn and leave rem sts on a spare needle.
Dec one st at beg of next and every foll alt row until 51(55) sts rem.
Cont without shaping until armhole measures the same as on Back, ending with a wrong-side row.
Shape Shoulder
Cast off 25(27) sts at beg of next row. Work one row, then cast off rem 26(28) sts.
Return to the sts on spare needle; with right side facing, sl first 29(31) sts on to a holder, rejoin yarn and patt to end.
Cont to match first side, reversing shaping.

NECKBAND
Join right shoulder seam.
With 2¾ mm needles and right side facing, pick up and K 30 sts evenly down left front neck, K front neck sts, pick up and K 29 sts evenly up right front neck, then K back neck sts. 143(147) sts.
Beg with a 2nd row, work 9 rows in rib as on Back.
Cast off **loosely** in rib.

ARMHOLE BORDERS
Join left shoulder and neckband seam.
With 2¾ mm needles and right side facing, pick up and K 143(149) sts evenly round armhole.
Beg with a 2nd row, work in rib as on Back for 3 cm/1¼ ins.
Cast off in rib.

TO MAKE UP
Press work lightly.
Join side seams.
Press seams.

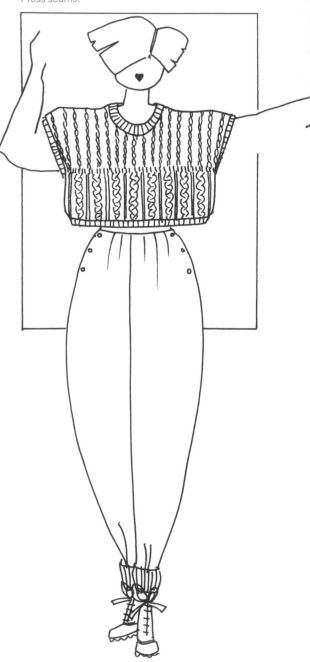

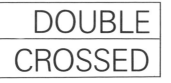

DOUBLE CROSSED

Materials
13(14:15) 50 g balls of *Patons Clansman DK* in main colour M.
1(2:2) balls in first contrast colour A.
2(2:2) balls in second contrast colour B.
1(1:1) ball in third contrast colour C.
1 pair each of 3¼ mm (No. 10) and 4 mm (No. 8) knitting needles.
4 buttons.

Measurements
Bust	86(91:97) cm	34(36:38) ins
Length	73 cm	28¾ ins
Sleeve Seam	47 cm	18½ ins

Tension 28 sts and 30 rows to 10 cm over cable patt on 4 mm needles.
25 sts and 30 rows to 10 cm over Fair Isle on 4 mm needles.

Abbreviations Alt-alternate; beg-beginning; cm-centimetres; cont-continue; dec-decrease; fol-following; ins-inches; inc-increase; K-knit; m 1-pick up loop lying between sts and work into the back of it; patt-pattern; P-purl; rem-remain; rep-repeat; sl-slip; st(s)-stitch(es): st st-stocking stitch.
Tw4-K into 4th st on left hand needle, then into 3rd st, then into 2nd st, then into first st and sl all 4 sts off needle together.

Note When working Fair Isle patt, strand yarn not in use loosely across wrong side of work.

BACK
With 3¼ mm needles and M, cast on 121(127:133) sts.
1st row (right side) K1, [P1, K1] to end.
2nd row P1, [K1, P1] to end.
Rep the last 2 rows 17 times more.
Next row Rib 3, inc in next st, [rib 4, inc in next st] 23(24:25) times, rib to end. 145(152:159) sts.
Change to 4 mm needles and cont in patt as folls:
* **1st row** K3(2:1), [P4, K5] to last 7(6:5) sts, P4, K to end.
2nd row P3(2:1), [K4, P5] to last 7(6:5) sts, K4, P to end.
Rep the last 2 rows once more, then the 1st row again. *
6th row P3(2:1), [Tw4, P5] to last 7(6:5) sts, Tw4, P to end.
Rep from * to * once.
12th row K9(8:6), [K2 tog, K7] 15(16:17) times, K1(0:0). 130(136:142) sts.
Beg with a P row, work 3 rows in st st.
16th row K0(1:0) A, 0(2:2) M, [2A, 2M] to last 2(1:0) sts, 2(1:0) A.
17th row P0(2:0) B, 2(3:0) M, [1M, 4B, 3M] to last 0(3:6) sts, 0(1:1) M, 0(2:4) B, 0(0:1) M.
18th row K0(0:1) C, 0(0:1) B, 0(1:2) C, 0(1:1) B, 0(1:1) C, [3C, 1B, 2C, 1B, 1C] to last 2(5:0) sts, 2(3:0) C, 0(1:0) B, 0(1:0) C.
19th row As 17th row.
20th row As 16th row.
With M only, work 5 rows in st st.
26th row As 16th row.
27th row P0(0:1) B, 0(2:4) M, 0(1:1) B, [3B, 4M, 1B] to last 2(5:0) sts, 2(3:0) B, 0(2:0) M.
28th row K2(2:0) C, 0(1:0) B, 0(2:0) C, [1B, 4C, 1B, 2C] to last 0(3:6) sts, 0(1:1) B, 0(2:4) C, 0(0:1) B.
29th row As 27th row.
30th row As 16th row.
With M only, work 4 rows in st st.
35th row With M, P9(8:6), [m 1, P8] 15(16:17) times, P to end. 145(152:159) sts.
36th row As 2nd row.
These 36 rows form the patt and are rep throughout. Cont

until 189 rows have been worked in patt.
Shape Shoulders
Cast off 25(27:28) sts at beg of next 2 rows, then 26(27:29) sts at beg of next 2 rows.
Cast off rem 43(44:45) sts.

LEFT FRONT
With 3¼ mm needles and M, cast on 93(97:99) sts and work 36 rows in rib as on Back.
Next row Rib 4(2:7), inc in next st, [rib 4(5:4), inc in next st] 15(14:15) times, rib to last 9 sts, turn and leave rem sts on a holder. 100(103:106) sts.
Change to 4 mm needles and cont in patt as folls:
1st row P0(2:0), K3(5:2), [P4, K5] to last 7(6:5) sts, P4, K to end.
Cont in patt as set, to match Back, dec one st at front edge on the 3rd and every foll 3rd row, until 49 sts in all have been dec at this edge, **at the same time**, dec 11 sts evenly across row 12, 10 sts across row 48, 9 sts across row 84, 6 sts across row 120 and 4 sts across row 156 of patt, (Note: the front edge dec has been included in these figures, i.e. on row 12, 10 sts across the row and one st at front edge) and inc 9 sts evenly across row 35, 8 sts across row 71, 7 sts across row 107 and 6 sts across rows 143 and 179. 51(54:57) sts.

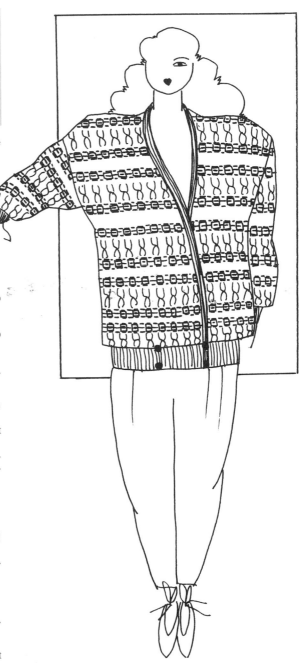

Cont without shaping until work measures the same as Back to shoulders, ending with a wrong-side row.
Shape Shoulder
Cast off 25(27:28) sts at beg of next row. Work one row, then cast off rem 26(27:29) sts.

RIGHT FRONT

With $3\frac{1}{4}$mm needles and M, cast on 93(97:99) sts and work 4 rows in rib as on Back.
** **Next row** Rib 5, cast off 4, rib 47(49:47) including st on needle after casting off, cast off 4, rib to end.
Next row Rib to end, casting on 4 sts over each 4 cast off. **
Work 24 rows.
Rep from ** to ** once.
Work 4 rows.
Next row Rib 9 sts and sl these on to a holder, rib 4(2:7), inc in next st, [rib 4(5:4), inc in next st] 15(14:15) times, rib to end. 100(103:106) sts.
Cont to match Left Front, reversing all shaping and position of patt as folls:
1st row K3(2:1), [P4, K5] to last 7(2:6) sts. P4(2:4), K3(0:2).

SLEEVES

With $3\frac{1}{4}$mm needles and M, cast on 63(65:67) sts and work 36 rows in rib as on Back, inc 10(8:15) sts evenly across the last row. 73(73:82) sts.
Change to 4 mm needles and cont in patt as given for the 1st size on Back, inc one st at each end of the 3rd and every foll 3rd row, working the inc sts into patt until 28(30:28) sts have been inc at each side, **at the same time**, dec 6 sts evenly across row 12, 9 sts across row 48 and 10 sts across row 84, (Note: the side incs have been included in these figures, i.e. on row 12, instead of inc one st at each end and dec 8 sts across the row we have dec 6) and inc 14 sts evenly across row 35 and 17 sts across row 71. 129(133:138) sts.
Cont without shaping until 106 rows have been worked in patt.
With M, P one row then cast off **loosely**.

LEFT FRONT BAND

Join shoulder seams.
With $3\frac{1}{4}$mm needles, M and right side facing, work in rib across sts on holder at beg of Left Front, working twice into first st. 10 sts.
Cont in rib until band, when slightly stretched, reaches up front edge and round to centre back neck.
Cast off in rib.

RIGHT FRONT BAND

With $3\frac{1}{4}$mm needles, M and wrong side facing, work in rib across sts on holder at beg of Right Front, working twice into first st. 10 sts.
Work to match Left Front Band.

TO MAKE UP

Press work according to instructions on ball band.
Sew in sleeves, with centre of sleeves to shoulder seams.
Join side and sleeve seams. Sew on front bands, joining ends at centre back neck.
Press seams.
Sew on buttons.

MOHAIR MAGIC

Materials

18(19:20) 25 g balls of *Hayfield Aspen Mohair*.
1 pair each of $4\frac{1}{2}$ mm (No. 7) and $5\frac{1}{2}$ mm (No. 5) knitting needles.

Measurements

Bust	86(91:97) cm	34(36:38) ins
Length	65(68:71) cm	$25\frac{1}{2}$($26\frac{3}{4}$:28) ins
Sleeve Seam	44 cm	$17\frac{1}{4}$ ins

Tension 15 sts and 20 rows to 10 cm over st st on $5\frac{1}{2}$ mm needles.

Abbreviations Alt-alternate; beg-beginning; cm-centimetres; cont-continue; dec-decrease; foll-following; ins-inches; inc-increase; K-knit; P-purl; rem-remain; rep-repeat; sl-slip; st(s)-stitch(es); st st-stocking stitch.

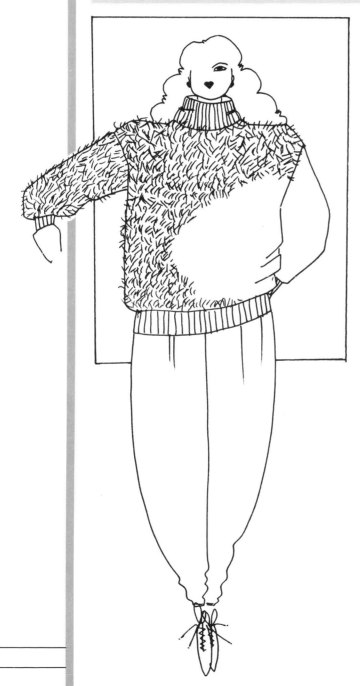

BACK

With $4\frac{1}{2}$ mm needles cast on 77(81:85) sts.
1st row K1, [P1, K1] to end.
2nd row P1, [K1, P1] to end.
Rep the last 2 rows until work measures 5 cm/2 ins from beg, ending with a 2nd row and inc one st in centre of last row. 78(82:86) sts.
Change to $5\frac{1}{2}$ mm needles and beg with a K row cont in st st until work measures 63(66:69) cm/$24\frac{3}{4}$(26:$27\frac{1}{4}$) ins from beg, ending with a P row.
Shape Neck
Next row K35(36:37), turn and leave rem sts on a spare needle.
Cast off 9 sts at beg of next row. Work 2 rows straight, then cast off rem 26(27:28) sts.
Return to the sts on spare needle; with right side facing, sl first 8(10:12) sts on to a holder, rejoin yarn, cast off 9 sts and K to end.
Cont to match first side, reversing shaping.

FRONT

Work as given for Back until work measures 58(61:64) cm/$22\frac{3}{4}$(24:$25\frac{1}{4}$) ins from beg, ending with a P row.
Shape Neck
Next row K35(36:37), turn and leave rem sts on a spare needle.
Cast off 3 sts at beg of next row, 2 sts at beg of foll 2 alt rows, then one st at beg of foll 2 alt rows. 26(27:28) sts.
Cont without shaping until work measures same as Back to shoulders, ending with a P row.
Cast off.
Return to the sts on spare needle; with right side facing, sl first 8(10:12) sts on to a holder, rejoin yarn, cast off 3 sts and K to end.
Cont to match first side, reversing shaping.

SLEEVES

With $4\frac{1}{2}$ mm needles cast on 39(41:43) sts and work in rib as on Back for 5 cm/2 ins, ending with a 1st row.
Next row Rib 1(2:3), [inc in next st, rib 5] 6 times, inc in next st, rib to end. 46(48:50) sts.
Change to $5\frac{1}{2}$ mm needles and beg with a K row, cont in st st inc one st at each end of the 5th and every foll 3rd row until there are 84(88:92) sts.
Cont without shaping until work measures 44 cm/$17\frac{1}{4}$ ins from beg, ending with a P row.
Cast off **loosely**.

COLLAR

Join left shoulder seam.
With $4\frac{1}{2}$ mm needles and right side facing, pick up and K 11 sts evenly down right back neck, K back neck sts, pick up and K 11 sts evenly up left back neck and 22 sts down left front neck, K front neck sts, then pick up and K 23 sts evenly up right front neck. 83(87:91) sts.
Beg with a 2nd row, work in rib as on Back for 8 cm/$3\frac{1}{4}$ ins.
Next row Rib 8(7:6), [work 3 times into next st, rib 10(11:12)] 6 times, work 3 times into next st, rib to end. 97(101:105) sts.
Cont in rib until collar measures 24 cm/$9\frac{1}{2}$ ins from beg.
Cast off **loosely** in rib.

TO MAKE UP

Do not press.
Join right shoulder and collar seam, reversing seam on collar to allow for turning. Sew in sleeves, with centre of sleeves to shoulder seams.
Join side and sleeve seams.

SKINNY RIB

Materials
8(8:9:9) 50 g balls of *Scheepjeswol Cotton Satin*.
1 pair each of 3 mm (No. 11) and 3¼ mm (No. 10) knitting needles.

Measurements
| Bust | 81(86:91:97) cm | 32(34:36:38) ins |
| Length | 48(50:52:54) cm | 19(19¾:20½:21¼) ins |

Tension 32 sts and 28 rows to 10 cm over rib on 3¼ mm needles.

> **Abbreviations** Alt-alternate; beg-beginning; cm-centimetres; cont-continue; dec-decrease; foll-following; ins-inches; inc-increase; K-knit; P-purl; rem-remain; rep-repeat; sl-slip; st(s)-stitch(es); tog-together.

BACK
With 3 mm needles cast on 111(119:127:135) sts.
1st row (right side) K1, [P1, K1] to end.
2nd row P1, [K1, P1] to end.
Rep the last 2 rows until work measures 7(8:9:10) cm/2¾(3¼:3½:4) ins from beg.
Change to 3¼ mm needles and cont in rib, inc one st at each end of the 5th and every foll 5th row until there are 131(139:147:155) sts.
Cont without shaping until work measures 26(27:28:29) cm/10¼(10¾:11:11½) ins from beg, ending with a wrong-side row.
Shape Armholes
Next row Work 3 tog, rib to last 3 sts, work 3 tog.
Next row Rib to end.
Next row Work 2 tog, rib to last 2 sts, work 2 tog.
Next row Rib to end.
Rep last 4 rows until 95(97:99:101) sts rem.
Work 1 row straight then dec one st at each end of the next and every foll alt row until 57(61:65:69) sts rem, ending with a wrong-side row.
Shape Neck
Next row Work 2 tog, rib 21(22:24:25), turn and leave rem sts on a spare needle.
Next row Cast off 10, rib to end.
Next row Work 2 tog, rib to end.
Next row Cast off 10, rib to end.
Cast off rem 1(2:4:5) sts.
Return to the sts on spare needle; with right side facing, sl first 11(13:13:15) sts on to a holder, rejoin yarn and rib to last 2 sts, work 2 tog.
Cont to match first side, reversing shaping.

FRONT
Work as given for Back until 71(75:79:83) sts rem, ending with a wrong-side row.
Shape Neck
Next row Work 2 tog, rib 28(29:31:32), turn and leave rem sts on a spare needle.
Next row Cast off 4, rib to end.
Next row Work 2 tog, rib to end.
Rep the last 2 rows twice more. 14(15:17:18) sts.
Next row Cast off 2, rib to end.
Next row Work 2 tog, rib to end.
Rep the last 2 rows once more, then the first of them again. 6(7:9:10) sts.
Dec one st at each end of the next and foll alt row. Work one row straight.
Dec one st at beg of next row. Work one row straight.
Cast off rem 1(2:4:5) sts.
Return to the sts on spare needle; with right side facing, sl first 11(13:13:15) sts on to a holder, rejoin yarn and rib to last 2 sts, work 2 tog.
Cont to match first side, reversing shaping.

COLLAR
Join left shoulder seam.
With 3 mm needles and right side facing, pick up and K 22 sts evenly down right back neck, K back neck sts, pick up and K 22 sts evenly up left back neck and 28 sts evenly down left front neck, K front neck sts, then pick up and K 29 sts evenly up right front neck. 123(127:127:131) sts.
Beg with a 2nd row, work in rib as on Back for 4 cm/1½ ins.
Next row Rib 2(4:4:2) [work 3 times into next st, rib 12(12:12:13)] 9 times, work 3 times into next st, rib to end. 143(147:147:151) sts. Cont in rib until Collar measures 8 cm/3¼ in from beg.
Change to 3¼ mm needles and cont until Collar measures 13 cm/5 ins from beg.
Cast off **loosely** in rib.

ARMHOLE BORDERS
Join right shoulder and collar seam, reversing seam on collar to allow for turning.
With 3 mm needles and right side facing, pick up and K 111(117:123:129) sts evenly round armhole.
Beg with a 2nd row, work 3 rows in rib as on Back. Cast off in rib.

TO MAKE UP
Do not press.
Join side seams.

ZANY ZIG ZAGS

Materials

13(15) 25 g hanks of *Rowan DK* in main colour M.
6(7) hanks in first contrast colour A.
5(6) hanks in second contrast colour B.
3(3) hanks in each of third and fourth contrast colours C and D.
1 pair each of 3¼ mm (No. 10) and 4 mm (No. 8) knitting needles.
3 buttons.

Measurements

Bust	81–91(97–107) cm	32–36(38–42) ins
Length	68(76) cm	26¾(30) ins
Sleeve Seam	50 cm	19¾ ins

Tension 24 sts and 29 rows to 10 cm over patt on 4 mm needles.

Abbreviations Alt-alternate; beg-beginning; cm-centimetres; cont-continue; dec-decrease; foll-following; ins-inches; inc-increase; K-knit; patt-pattern; P-purl; rem-remain; rep-repeat; sl-slip; st(s)-stitch(es); st st-stocking stitch.

Note When working in patt, on rows 1–4, strand yarn not in use loosely across wrong side of work, weaving it in when working across 5 or more sts, on rows 5–22, use a separate length of yarn for each section and twist yarns together on every row to avoid a hole. Due to the nature of patt, it is only possible to give 2 sets of figures to cover 6 bust sizes. The actual size of the garment is 104(121) cm/ 41(47½) ins all round. By giving these figures we hope it will help you to choose which size is more suitable to your needs.

BACK

With 3¼ mm needles and M, cast on 121(141) sts.
1st row K1, [P1, K1] to end.
2nd row P1, [K1, P1] to end.
Rep the last 2 rows 4 times more.
Change to 4 mm needles. Beg with a K row and working in st st throughout, cont in patt from chart until 184(206) rows have been worked in patt.

Shape Neck

Keeping patt correct;
Next row Patt 53(62), cast off 15(17), patt to end.
Cont on last set of sts only, work one row.
Cast off 4 sts at beg of next and foll 2 alt rows.
Cast off rem 41(50) sts.
Return to the sts which were left; with wrong side facing, rejoin yarns, cast off 4 sts and patt to end.
Cont to match first side reversing shaping.

LEFT FRONT

With 3¼ mm needles and M, cast on 71(81) sts and work 10 rows in rib as on Back.
Change to 4 mm needles. Beg with a K row and working in st st throughout, cont as folls:
Next row K to last 10 sts, working in patt as first row of chart, turn and leave rem sts on a holder. 61(71) sts.
Cont in patt from chart until 48 rows have been worked in patt.

Shape Front Edge

Keeping patt correct, dec one st at end of next row and at this same edge on every foll 7th row until 41(50) sts rem.
Cont until 190(212) rows have been worked in patt.
Cast off.

RIGHT FRONT

With 3¼ mm needles and M, cast on 71(81) sts and work 6 rows in rib as on Back.
Next row Rib 3, cast off 3, rib to end.
Next row Rib to end casting on 3 sts over the 3 cast off.
Work 2 more rows in rib.

Next row Rib 10 and sl these sts on to a holder, change to 4 mm needles and K to end working in patt as first row of chart.
Cont in patt from chart to match Left Front, reversing shaping.

SLEEVES

With 3¼ mm needles and M, cast on 51(55) sts and work 10 rows in rib as on Back, inc 10(12) sts evenly across the last row. 61(67) sts.
Change to 4 mm needles. Beg with a K row and working in st st throughout, cont in patt from chart, inc one st at each end of the 3rd and every foll 4th row, working the inc sts into patt, until there are 119(125) sts. Cont without shaping until 136 rows have been worked in patt. Cast off **loosely**.

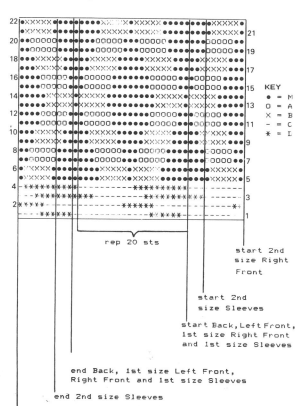

```
rep 20 sts

KEY
● = M
○ = A
X = B
— = C
✻ = D
```

start 2nd size Right Front

start 2nd size Sleeves

start Back, Left Front, 1st size Right Front and 1st size Sleeves

end Back, 1st size Left Front, Right Front and 1st size Sleeves

end 2nd size Sleeves

end 2nd size Left Front

BUTTON BAND

Join shoulder seams.
With 3¼ mm needles, M and right side facing, work in rib across sts on holder at beg of Left Front, working twice into the first st. 11 sts.
Cont in rib until band, when slightly stretched reaches up front edge and round to centre back neck.
Cast off in rib.
Tack band in place and with pins mark the positions of buttons; 1st to come level with buttonhole already worked, 2nd will be just below beg of front shaping with one more spaced halfway between these 2.

BUTTONHOLE BAND

With 3¼ mm needles, M and wrong side facing, work in rib across sts on holder at beg of Right Front, working twice into the first st. 11 sts.
Work as given for Button Band, making buttonholes as before to correspond with positions of pins.

TO MAKE UP

Press work lightly. Sew in sleeves, with centre of sleeves to shoulder seams. Join side and sleeve seams. Sew on front bands, joining at centre back neck. Press seams. Sew on buttons.

SOFTLY CABLED

Materials
10(10:11:11) 50 g balls of *Patons Solo*.
1 pair each of 5 mm (No. 6) and 6 mm (No. 4) knitting needles.
1 cable needle.

Measurements
Bust	81(86:91:97) cm	32(34:36:38) ins
Length	58(59:60:61) cm	$22\frac{3}{4}(23\frac{1}{4}:23\frac{1}{2}:24)$ ins

Tension 20 sts and 24 rows to 10 cm over patt on 6 mm needles.

Abbreviations Alt-alternate; beg-beginning; cm-centimetres; cont-continue; dec-decrease; foll-following; g st-garter stitch; ins-inches; inc-increase; K-knit; patt-pattern; P-purl; rem-remain; rep-repeat; sl-slip; st(s)-stitch(es).
C8-sl next 4 sts to cable needle to front of work, K4, then K4 from cable needle.

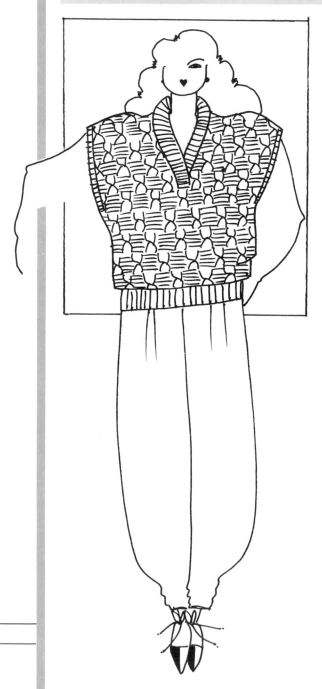

FRONT
With 5 mm needles cast on 66(70:74:78) sts.
1st row (right side) K2, [P2, K2] to end.
2nd row P2, [K2, P2] to end.
Rep the last 2 rows until work measures 9 cm/$3\frac{1}{2}$ ins from beg, ending with a 1st row.
Next row Rib 3(5:7:9), [(inc in next st) 3 times, rib 1] 15 times, inc in next st, rib to end. 112(116:120:124) sts.
Change to 6 mm needles and cont in patt as folls:
1st row K to end.
2nd row K4(6:8:10), [P8, K8] 6 times, P8, K to end.
Rep the last 2 rows twice more.
7th row K4(6:8:10), [C8, K8] 6 times, C8, K to end.
8th row As 2nd row.
Rep 1st and 2nd rows twice more.
13th row K to end.
14th row K12(14:16:18), [P8, K8] 6 times, K to end.
Rep the last 2 rows twice more.
19th row K12(14:16:18), [C8, K8] 6 times, K to end.
20th row As 14th row.
Rep 13th and 14th rows twice more.
These 24 rows form the patt and are rep throughout. ******
Work 48 more rows in patt. Place a marker at each end of last row.
Divide for Neck
Keeping patt correct;
Next row Patt 52(54:56:58), turn and leave rem sts on a spare needle.
Next row Patt to end.
Dec one st at end of next and every foll 4th row until 42(44:46:48) sts rem.
Cont without shaping until work measures 58(59:60:61) cm/$22\frac{3}{4}(23\frac{1}{4}:23\frac{1}{2}:24)$ ins from beg, ending with a wrong-side row.
Shape Shoulder
Cast off 14(15:15:16) sts at beg of next and foll alt row.
Work one row, then cast off rem 14(14:16:16) sts.
Return to the sts which were left; with right side facing, sl first 8 sts on to a holder, rejoin yarn and patt to end.
Cont to match first side, reversing shaping.

BACK
Work as given for Front to ******.
Cont without shaping until work measures the same as Front to shoulders, ending with a wrong-side row.
Shape Shoulders
Cast off 14(15:15:16) sts at beg of next 4 rows, then 14(14:16:16) sts at beg of next 2 rows.
Cast off rem 28 sts.

NECKBAND
Join shoulder seams.
With 5 mm needles and right side facing, K across sts on holder, knitting 2 tog at end of row. 7 sts.
Cont in g st until band, when slightly stretched, fits up left front, round back neck and down right front.
Cast off.

TO MAKE UP
Do not press.
Join side seams to markers. Sew neckband to neck edge, sewing cast off edge behind centre front sts which were left on holder.

Materials
11(11:12) 50 g balls of *Emu Superwash* 4 ply.
1 pair each of 2¾ mm (No. 12) and 3¼ mm (No. 10) knitting needles.
1 cable needle.

Measurements
Bust	86(91:97) cm	34(36:38) ins
Length	54(55:56) cm	21¼(21¾:22) ins
Sleeve Seam	47 cm	18½ ins

Tension 33 sts and 37 rows to 10 cm over patt on 3¼ mm needles.

Abbreviations Alt-alternate; beg-beginning; cm-centimetres; cont-continue; dec-decrease; foll-following; ins-inches; inc-increase; K-knit; m 1-pick up loop lying between sts and work into the back of it; patt-pattern; P-purl; P1B-P1 through back of loop; psso-pass the slipped stitch over; rem-remain; rep-repeat; sl-slip; st(s)-stitch(es); tog-together; yfwd-yarn forward; yon-yarn over needle; yrn-yarn round needle.
C6B-sl next 3 sts to cable needle to back of work, K3, then K3 from cable needle.
C6F-sl next 3 sts to cable needle to front of work, K3, then K3 from cable needle.
MB-[K1, P1, K1, P1, K1] into next st, turn, K5, turn, P5, turn, K2 tog, K1, K2 tog, turn, K3 tog.

BACK
With 2¾ mm needles cast on 119(127:135) sts.
1st row (right side) K1, [P1, K1] to end.
2nd row P1, [K1, P1] to end.
Rep the last 2 rows until work measures 7 cm/2¾ ins from beg, ending with a 1st row.
Next row Rib 17(20:22), m 1, [rib 2, m 1] 43(43:45) times, rib to end. 163(171:181) sts.
Change to 3¼ mm needles and cont in patt as folls:
1st row P5(9:1), K1, [sl 1, K1, psso, yfwd, C6B, K6] 4(4:5) times, P2(2:1), K3, K2 tog, P3, K1, yrn, P8, MB, P8, yon, K1, P3, sl 1, K1, psso, K3, * P2(2:1), K1, [sl 1, K1, psso, yfwd, C6B, K6] 4(4:5) times, P5(9:1) *.
2nd row K6(10:2), [P2 tog, yrn, P11, K1] 4(4:5) times, K4(4:3), P2, K3, P2, K8, P1B, K8, P2, K3, P2, K5(5:4), * [P2 tog, yrn, P11, K1] 4(4:5) times, K5(9:1). *
3rd row P5(9:1), K1, [sl 1, K1, psso, yfwd, K12] 4(4:5) times, P2(2:1), K4, P2 tog, P1, K1, yrn, P5, MB, P3, K1, P3, MB, P5, yon, K1, P1, P2 tog, K4, * P2(2:1), K1, [sl 1, K1, psso, yfwd, K12] 4(4:5) times, P5(9:1). *
4th row Patt 62(66:72) as 2nd row, K2(2:1), [K2, P2] twice, K5, P1B, K3, P1, K3, P1B, K5, [P2, K2] twice, K3(3:2), work from * to * on 2nd row.
5th row P5(9:1), K1, [sl 1, K1, psso, yfwd, K3, C6F, K3] 4(4:5) times, P2(2:1), K4, P2 tog, K1, yrn, P2, MB, [P3, K1] 3 times, P3, MB, P2, yon, K1, P2 tog, K4, * P2(2:1), K1, [sl 1, K1, psso, yfwd, K3, C6F, K3] 4(4:5) times, P5(9:1). *
6th row Patt 68(72:77) as 2nd row, K1, P2, K2, P1B, [K3, P1] 3 times, K3, P1B, K2, P2, K1, P2, K5(5:4), work from * to * on 2nd row.
7th row Patt 68(72:77) as 3rd row, K2 tog, yrn, [P3, K1] 5 times, P3, yon, sl 1, K1, psso, K4, work from * to * on 3rd row.
8th row Patt 66(70:75) as 2nd row, P4, [K3, P1] 5 times, K3, P4, K5(5:4), work from * to * on 2nd row.
9th row Patt 69(73:78) as 1st row, yrn, K3, K1, P1, P2 tog, K1, P2 tog, P1, K1, P3, K1, yrn, P4, yon, sl 1, K1, psso, K3, rep from * to * on 1st row.
10th row Patt 66(70:75) as 2nd row, P3, K4, P2, K3, [P1, K2] twice, P1, K3, P2, K4, P3, K5(5:4), work from * to * on 2nd row.
11th row Patt 64(68:73) as 3rd row, K2, K2 tog, yrn, P6, yon, K1, P3, [K1, P2 tog] twice, K1, P3, K1, yrn, P6, yon, sl 1, K1, psso, K2, work from * to * on 3rd row.
12th row Patt 62(66:72) as 2nd row, K12(12:11), P2, K3, [P1, K1] twice, P1, K3, P2, K13(13:12), work from * to * on 2nd row.
13th row Patt 64(68:73) as 5th row, K2, MB, P8, yon, K1, P3, sl 1, K1, psso, K1, K2 tog, P3, K1, yrn, P8, MB, K2, work from * to * on 5th row.
14th row Patt 66(70:75) as 2nd row, P1B, K8, P2, K3, P3, K3, P2, K8, P1B, K5(5:4), work from * to * on 2nd row.
15th row Patt 64(68:73) as 3rd row, K3, P3, MB, P5, yon, K1, P1, P2 tog, K3, P2 tog, P1, K1, yrn, P5, MB, P3, K3, work from * to * on 3rd row.
16th row Patt 66(70:75) as 2nd row, P1, K3, P1B, K5, P2, K2, P3, K2, P2, K5, P1B, K3, P1, K5(5:4), work from * to * on 2nd row.
17th row Patt 67(71:76) as set, P3, K1, P3, MB, P2, yon, K1, P2 tog, K3, P2 tog, K1, yrn, P2, MB, P3, K1, P3, K3, patt to end as set.
18th row Patt 66(70:75), [P1, K3] twice, P1B, K2, P2, K1, P3, K1, P2, K2, P1B, [K3, P1] twice, patt to end.
19th row Patt 64(68:73), K3, [P3, K1] twice, P3, yon, sl 1, K1, psso, K3, K2 tog, yrn, [P3, K1] twice, P3, K3, patt to end.
20th row Patt 66(70:75), [P1, K3] 3 times, P7, [K3, P1] 3 times, patt to end.

21st row Patt 64(68:73), K3, P2 tog, P1, K1, P3, K1, yrn, P4, yon, sl 1, K1, psso, K1, K2 tog, yrn, P4, yon, K1, P3, K1, P1, P2 tog, K3, patt to end.

22nd row Patt 62(66:72), K2(2:1), [K2, P1] twice, K3, P2, K4, P5, K4, P2, K3, [P1, K2] twice, patt to end.

23rd row Patt 64(68:73), K3, P2 tog, K1, P3, K1, yrn, P6, yon, sl 1, K2 tog, psso, yrn, P6, yon, K1, P3, K1, P2 tog, K3, patt to end.

24th row Patt 66(70:75), P1, K1, P1, K3, P2, K15, P2, K3, P1, K1, P1, patt to end.

These 24 rows form the patt and are rep throughout. Cont in patt until work measures 54(55:56) cm/21¼(21¾:22) ins from beg, ending with a wrong-side row.

Shape Shoulders

Cast off 19(20:21) sts at beg of next 4 rows, then 18(19:21) sts at beg of next 2 rows.

Leave rem 51(53:55) sts on a holder.

FRONT

Work as given for Back until work measures 48(49:50) cm/ 19(19¼:19¾) ins from beg, ending with a wrong-side row.

Shape Neck

Keeping patt correct;

Next row Patt 72(75:79), turn and leave rem sts on a spare needle.

Dec one st at beg of next row and at this same edge on every foll row until 56(59:63) sts rem.

Cont without shaping until work measures the same as Back to shoulders, ending with a wrong-side row.

Shape Shoulders

Cast off 19(20:21) sts at beg of next and foll alt row. Work one row, then cast off rem 18(19:21) sts.

Return to the sts on spare needle; with right side facing, sl first 19(21:23) sts on to a holder, rejoin yarn and patt to end.

Cont to match first side, reversing shaping.

SLEEVES

With 2¾ mm needles cast on 53(55:57) sts and work in rib as on Back for 6 cm/2¼ ins, ending with a 1st row.

Next row Rib 11(12:13), m 1, [rib 1, m 1] 31 times, rib to end. 85(87:89) sts.

Change to 3¼ mm needles and cont in patt as folls:

1st row K11(12:13), sl 1, K1, psso, yfwd, C6B, K9, K2 tog, P3, K1, yrn, P8, MB, P8, yon, K1, P3, sl 1, K1, psso, K4, sl 1, K1, psso, yfwd, C6B, K6, sl 1, K1, psso, yfwd, C6B, K2(3:4).

2nd row P10(11:12), K1, P2 tog, yrn, P11, [K3, P2] twice, K8, P1B, K8, [P2, K3] twice, P2 tog, yrn, P11, K1, P2 tog, yrn, P8(9:10).

Cont in patt as set, to match Back, inc one st at each end of the 3rd and every foll 4th row, working the inc sts into patt, until there are 137(143:149) sts.

Cont without shaping until work measures 47 cm/18½ ins from beg, ending with a wrong-side row.

Cast off **loosely**.

NECKBAND

Join right shoulder seam.

With 2¾ mm needles and right side facing, pick up and K 22 sts evenly down left front neck, K front neck sts, inc one st in centre, pick up and K 22 sts evenly up right front neck, then K back neck sts, inc 2 sts evenly across them. 117(121:125) sts.

Beg with a 2nd row, work in rib as on Back for 8 cm/3¼ ins.

Cast off **loosely** in rib.

TO MAKE UP

Press work lightly according to instructions on ball band. Join left shoulder and neckband seam. Sew in sleeves, with centre of sleeves to shoulder seams. Join side and sleeve seams. Fold neckband in half to inside and sl st. Press seams.

LEAN AND LINEN LOOK

Materials
10(11:11:12) 50 g balls of *Scheepjeswol Granada Cotton*.
1 pair each of $3\frac{1}{4}$ mm (No. 10) and $3\frac{3}{4}$ mm (No. 9) knitting needles.
3 buttons.

Measurements
Bust	81(86:91:97) cm	32 (34:36:38) ins
Length	73(75:77:79) cm	$28\frac{3}{4}$ ($29\frac{1}{2}$:$30\frac{1}{4}$:31) ins

Tension 23 sts and 30 rows to 10 cm over st st on $3\frac{3}{4}$ mm needles.

Abbreviations Alt-alternate; beg-beginning; cm-centimetres; cont-continue; foll-following; g st-garter stitch; ins-inches; inc-increase; K-knit; patt-pattern; P-purl; rem-remain; rep-repeat; st(s)-stitch(es); st st-stocking stitch.

BACK
With $3\frac{1}{4}$ mm needles cast on 119(123:129:135) sts.
1st row K1, [P1, K1] to end.
2nd row P1, [K1, P1] to end.

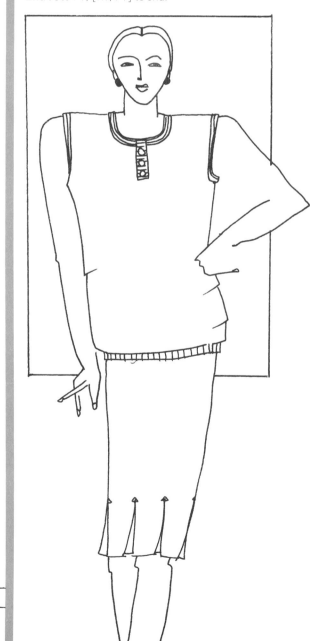

Rep the last 2 rows 4 times more, inc one st in centre of the last row. 120(124:130:136) sts.
Change to $3\frac{3}{4}$ mm needles and beg with a K row cont in st st until work measures 48(49:50:51) cm/19($19\frac{1}{4}$:$19\frac{3}{4}$:20) ins from beg, ending with a P row.

Shape Armholes
Cast off 6(6:7:8) sts at beg of next 2 rows 108(112:116:120) sts. **
Cont without shaping until armholes measure 15(16:17:18) cm/6($6\frac{1}{4}$:$6\frac{3}{4}$:7) ins, ending with a P row.
Cont in patt as folls:
1st row K51(53:55:57), P6, K to end.
2nd and every foll alt row P to end.
3rd row K48(50:52:54), P12, K to end.
5th row K45(47:49:51), P18, K to end.
7th row K43(45:47:49), P22, K to end.
9th row K41(43:45:47), P26, K to end.
11th row K39(41:43:45), P30, K to end.
13th row K38(40:42:44), P32, K to end.
Cont as set, working 2 more sts into g st on every alt row until there are 42 sts being worked in centre panel, ending with a wrong-side row. Rep the last 2 rows 3 times more.

Shape Shoulders
Cast off 33(35:37:39) sts at beg of next 2 rows.
Leave rem 42 sts on a holder.

FRONT
Work as given for Back to **.
Cont without shaping until armholes measure 7 cm/$2\frac{3}{4}$ ins, ending with a P row.

Divide for Front Opening
Next row K51(53:55:57), cast off 6, K to end.
Cont on last set of sts only without shaping until armhole measures 19(20:21:22) cm/$7\frac{1}{2}$($7\frac{3}{4}$:$8\frac{1}{4}$:$8\frac{3}{4}$) ins, ending with a P row.

Shape Neck
Cast off 4 sts at beg of next row, 3 sts at beg of foll 2 alt rows, 2 sts at beg of foll 3 alt rows, then one st at beg of foll 2 alt rows. 33(35:37:39) sts.
Cont without shaping until armhole measures the same as on Back, ending with a K row.
Cast off.
Return to the sts which were left; with wrong side facing, rejoin yarn and P to end.
Cont to match first side, reversing shaping.

BUTTON BAND
With $3\frac{1}{4}$ mm needles cast on 10 sts and work in g st until band, when slightly stretched reaches up front opening, ending with a wrong-side row.
Leave sts on a holder.
Tack band in place and with pins mark the positions of buttons; 1st to come 1 cm/$\frac{1}{2}$ in from lower edge, 2nd will be 1 cm/$\frac{1}{2}$ in down from neck edge with one more spaced halfway between these 2.

BUTTONHOLE BAND
Work as given for Button Band, making buttonholes to correspond with positions of pins as folls:
(right side) K3, cast off 4, K to end.
Next row K to end, casting on 4 sts over the 4 cast off.

NECKBAND
Join shoulder seams.
With $3\frac{1}{4}$ mm needles and right side facing, K 10 sts of Buttonhole Band, pick up and K 28 sts evenly up right front neck, K back neck sts, pick up and K 28 sts evenly down left front neck, then K 10 sts of Button Band.
Work 6 rows in g st, then cast off.

ARMHOLE BORDERS
With $3\frac{1}{4}$ mm needles and right side facing, pick up and K 113(117:121:125) sts evenly round armhole.
Work 6 rows in g st, then cast off.

TO MAKE UP
Press work according to instructions on ball band.
Join side seams. Sew on front bands, sewing ends of bands to the cast off sts at centre front.
Press seams.
Sew on buttons.

SITTING PRETTY

Materials
10(11:11) 50 g balls of *Naturally Beautiful Cotton Cable*.
1 pair each of $2\frac{3}{4}$ mm (No. 12) and $3\frac{1}{4}$ mm (No. 10) knitting needles.
Set of four $2\frac{3}{4}$ mm double pointed needles.
1 cable needle.

Measurements
Bust	86(91:97) cm	34(36:38) ins
Length	48(49:50) cm	19(19$\frac{1}{4}$:19$\frac{3}{4}$) ins
Sleeve Seam	44(45:46) cm	17$\frac{1}{4}$(17$\frac{3}{4}$:18) ins

Tension 36 sts and 40 rows to 10 cm over patt on $3\frac{1}{4}$ mm needles.

Abbreviations Alt-alternate; beg-beginning; cm-centimetres; cont-continue; dec-decrease; foll-following; ins-inches; inc-increase; K-knit; m 1-pick up the loop lying between the sts and work into the back of it; patt-pattern; P-purl; rem-remain; rep-repeat; sl-slip; st(s)-stitch(es).
C3B-sl next st to cable needle to back of work, K2, then K1 from cable needle.
C3F-sl next 2 sts to cable needle to front of work, K1, then K2 from cable needle.
T3B-sl next st to cable needle to back of work, K2, then P1 from cable needle.
T3F-sl next 2 sts to cable needle to front of work, P1, then K2 from cable needle.
C4B-sl next 2 sts to cable needle to back of work, K2, then K2 from cable needle.
C4F-sl next 2 sts to cable needle to front of work, K2, then K2 from cable needle.

PANEL A (26 sts)
1st row P4, C3B, K12, C3F, P4.
2nd row K4, P18, K4.
3rd row P3, C3B, K4, T3B, T3F, K4, C3F, P3.
4th row K3, P9, K2, P9, K3.
5th row P2, C3B, K4, T3B, P2, T3F, K4, C3F, P2.
6th row K2, P9, K4, P9, K2.
7th row P1, C3B, K4, T3B, P4, T3F, K4, C3F, P1.
8th row K1, P9, K6, P9, K1.
9th row C3B, K4, T3B, P6, T3F, K4, C3F.
10th row P9, K8, P9.
11th row K6, T3B, P8, T3F, K6.
12th row P8, K10, P8.
13th row K6, C3F, P8, C3B, K6.
14th row As 10th row.
15th row T3F, K4, C3F, P6, C3B, K4, T3B.
16th row As 8th row.
17th row P1, T3F, K4, C3F, P4, C3B, K4, T3B, P1.
18th row As 6th row.
19th row P2, T3F, K4, C3F, P2, C3B, K4, T3B, P2.
20th row As 4th row.
21st row P3, T3F, K4, C3F, C3B, K4, T3B, P3.
22nd row As 2nd row.
23rd row P4, T3F, K12, T3B, P4.
24th row K5, P16, K5.
These 24 rows form rep of patt.

PANEL B (10 sts)
1st row P1, K8, P1.
2nd and every foll alt row K1, P8, K1.
3rd row P1, C4B, C4F, P1.
5th row As 1st row.
7th row P1, C4F, C4B, P1.
9th row As 1st row.
11th row As 7th row.
13th row As 1st row.
15th row As 3rd row.
16th row As 2nd row.
These 16 rows form the rep of patt.

PANEL C (6 sts)
1st row P1, K4, P1.
2nd row K1, P4, K1.
3rd row P1, C4F, P1.
4th row As 2nd row.
5th row As 1st row.
6th row As 2nd row.
These 6 rows form the rep of patt.

BACK
With $2\frac{3}{4}$ mm needles cast on 111(119:125) sts.
1st row (right side) K1, [P1, K1] to end.
2nd row P1, [K1, P1] to end.
Rep the last 2 rows until work measures 6 cm/$2\frac{1}{4}$ ins from beg, ending with a 1st row.
Next row Rib 14(18:16), m 1, [rib 2, m 1] 42(42:46) times, rib to end. 154(162:172) sts.
Change to $3\frac{1}{4}$ mm needles and cont in patt as folls:
1st row P3(7:2), [work as 1st row of Panel B] 0(0:1) time, [work as 1st row of Panel C, Panel B] 3 times, [work as 1st row of Panel A] twice, [work as 1st row of Panel B, Panel C] 3 times, [work as 1st row of Panel B] 0(0:1) time, P to end.
2nd row K3(7:2), [work as 2nd row of Panel B] 0(0:1) time, [work as 2nd row of Panel C, Panel B] 3 times, [work as 2nd row of Panel A] twice, [work as 2nd row of Panel B, Panel C] 3 times, [work as 2nd row of Panel B] 0(0:1) time, K to end.
Cont in patt as set, until work measures 31 cm/$12\frac{1}{4}$ ins from beg, ending with a wrong-side row.
Shape Armholes
Keeping patt correct, cast off 5(5:6) sts at beg of next 2 rows.
Dec one st at each end of the next and every foll alt row until 94(100:106) sts rem, ending with a wrong-side row. **
Work 18 rows straight.
Shape Shoulders
Cast off 11(12:13) sts at beg of next 4 rows.
Leave rem 50(52:54) sts on a holder.

FRONT
Work as given for Back to **.
Shape Neck
Keeping patt correct;
Next row Patt 38(40:42), turn and leave rem sts on a spare needle.
Dec one st at neck edge on next 16 rows. 22(24:26) sts.
Work one row straight.
Shape Shoulder
Cast off 11(12:13) sts at beg of next row. Work one row, then cast off rem 11(12:13) sts.
Return to the sts on spare needle; with right side facing, sl first 18(20:22) sts on to a holder, rejoin yarn and patt to end.
Cont to match first side, reversing shaping.

SLEEVES
With $2\frac{3}{4}$ mm needles cast on 61(63:65) sts and work in rib as on Back for 6 cm/$2\frac{1}{4}$ ins, ending with a 1st row.
Next row Rib 4(4:2), m 1, [rib 2, m 1] 26(28:30) times, rib to end 88(92:96) sts.
Change to $3\frac{1}{4}$ mm needles and cont in patt as folls:
1st row P5(1:3), [work as 1st row of Panel B] 1(0:0) time, [work as 1st row of Panel C, Panel B] 1(2:2) times, work as 1st row of Panel A, [work as 1st row of Panel B, Panel C] 1(2:2) times, [work as 1st row of Panel B] 1(0:0) time, P to end.
2nd row K5(1:3), [work as 2nd row of Panel B] 1(0:0) time, [work as 2nd row of Panel C, Panel B] 1(2:2) times, work as 2nd row of Panel A, [work as 2nd row of Panel B, Panel C] 1(2:2) times, [work as 2nd row of Panel B] 1(0:0) time, K to end.
Cont in patt as set, inc one st at each end of the 5th and every foll 4th row, working the inc sts into patt, until there are 138(142:148) sts.
Cont without shaping until work measures 44(45:46) cm/$17\frac{1}{4}$(17$\frac{3}{4}$:18) ins from beg, ending with a wrong-side row.
Shape Top
Keeping patt correct, cast off 5(5:6) sts at beg of next 2 rows.

Dec one st at each end of the next and every foll row until 30 sts rem, ending with a wrong-side row.
Cast off **loosely**.

COLLAR

Join shoulder seams.
With set of four 2¾ mm needles and right side facing, pick up and K 26 sts down left front neck, K front neck sts, inc 2 sts evenly across them, pick up and K 26 sts evenly up right front neck, then K back neck sts, inc 6 sts evenly across them. 128(132:136) sts.
Work 5 cm/2 ins in rounds of K1, P1 rib.
Next row Rib to centre front, turn.
Cont working in **rows**, until Collar measures 8 cm/3¼ ins.
Dec one st at each end of next and foll 3 alt rows.
Work one row straight, then dec one st at each end of next 10 rows.
Cast off **loosely** in rib.

TO MAKE UP

Press work according to instructions on ball band.
Sew in sleeves. Join side and sleeve seams.
Press seams.

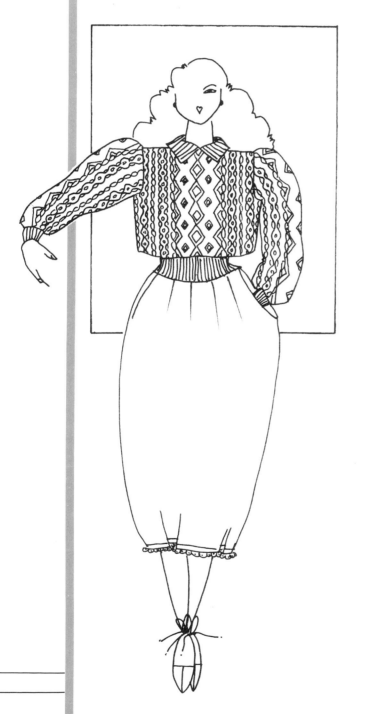

ACKNOWLEDGEMENTS

The publishers would like to thank the following for their assistance:

Pat Menchini
Gaye Hawkins
Sue Roberts
Mrs K Murphy
Mrs B Webb
Milly Johnson
Grace Paull
Vera Moore
Isabel Kemp
Mrs Stenning
Mrs Matthews
Mrs Kingman
Mrs Neville
Mary McHugh
Mrs Badrick
Mrs Tracy
Miss K Brittain
Mrs M Coles

Clothes and accessories by: Benetton; Fenn Wright & Manson; Georges Rech; In Wear; Laura Ashley; Liberty; Mulberry; New Man; Palladium; Peepers; Ralph Lauren; Strawberry Studio.

Argyll Wools Ltd
P.O. Box 15
Priestley Mills
Pudsey
West Yorkshire
LS28 9LT

0532 558411

Emu Wools Ltd
Leeds Road
Greengates
Bradford
West Yorkshire
BD10 9TE

0274 614031

French Wools Ltd
(Pingouin)
7–11 Lexington Street
London
W1R 4BU

493 4477

Hayfield Textiles Ltd
Hayfields Mills
Glusburn
Nr Keighley
West Yorkshire
BD20 8QP

0535 33333

Naturally Beautiful
Main Street
Dent Sedbergh
Cumbria
LA10 5QL

05875 421

Patons and Baldwins Ltd
Alloa
Clackmannanshire
Scotland

0259 723431

Rowan
Green Lane Mill
Washpit
Holmfirth
West Yorkshire
HD7 1RW

0484 686714

Scheepjeswol UK Ltd
7 Colemeadow Road
Redditch
Worcestershire

0527 61056

Sirdar PLC
Flanshaw Lane
Alverthorpe
Wakefield
West Yorkshire
WF2 9ND

0924 371501

W. H. Smith Woolshops
Strand House
Greenbridge Industrial Estate
Greenbridge Road
Swindon
SN3 3LD

0793 616161

3 Suisses
Marlborough House
38 Welford Road
Leicester
LE2 7AA

0533 554713

Sunbeam Knitting Wools
Crawshaw Mills
Pudsey
West Yorkshire
LS28 7BS

0532 571871

Viking Wools Ltd
(Berger du Nord)
Rothay Holme
Ambleside
Cumbria

0966 32991

Wendy Wools
Carter and Parker Ltd
Gordon Mills
Netherfield Road
Guiseley
Leeds
LS20 9PD

0943 72264